BLOOD
AND
GERMS

THE CIVIL WAR BATTLE
AGAINST WOUNDS AND DISEASE

BLOOD

AND

GERMS

THE CIVIL WAR BATTLE
AGAINST WOUNDS AND DISEASE

BY

GAIL JARROW

CALKINS CREEK
AN IMPRINT OF BOYDS MILLS & KANE
NEW YORK

For information about permission to reproduce selections from this book,
please contact permissions@bmkbooks.com.

Calkins Creek
An imprint of Boyds Mills & Kane, a division of Astra Publishing House
calkinscreekbooks.com
Printed in China

ISBN: 978-1-68437-176-1
Library of Congress Control Number: 2019953787

First edition
10 9 8 7 6 5 4 3 2 1

Design by Red Herring Design
The text is set in ITC Century.
The titles are set in Eveleth.

TABLE OF CONTENTS

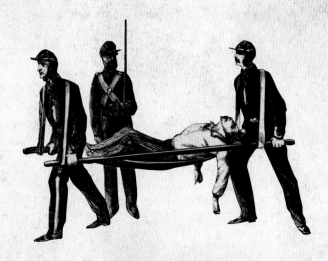

DEDICATED TO three Civil War soldiers—
George, Henry, and Jacob.
If they hadn't survived the blood and germs,
this book wouldn't have been written.

THE STATES TAKE SIDES

UNION STATES

Maine
New Hampshire
Vermont
Massachusetts
Rhode Island
Connecticut
New York
New Jersey
Pennsylvania
Ohio
Michigan
Indiana
Illinois
Wisconsin
Minnesota
Iowa
Kansas
Oregon
California
Nevada (new state admitted
    to Union in 1864)
* West Virginia (new state
    admitted to Union in 1863)
* Delaware
* Maryland
* Kentucky
* Missouri

CONFEDERATE STATES

Virginia
North Carolina
South Carolina
Georgia
Florida
Tennessee
Arkansas
Alabama
Mississippi
Louisiana
Texas

* Border States that held slaves but stayed in the Union.
Some residents chose to fight with the Confederate Army.

BEFORE YOU READ ON...

Blood and Germs is the story of medicine during the Civil War, a conflict that involved as many as 4 million American men. Because the war was fought mainly on land, the majority of them were army soldiers, far outnumbering navy sailors. My story focuses on the armies.

In July 1862, the Union army began allowing African Americans to enlist, and in May 1863, it established the United States Colored Troops. Some black men were already sailors in the U.S. Navy. Many who volunteered lived in the North. Others were

Union (left) and Confederate soldiers

Union (left) and Confederate sailors

A black soldier (left) and sailor who served in the Union's military.

former slaves who escaped to Union-controlled areas of the South. During the Civil War, approximately 180,000 African American men served as soldiers and 20,000 as sailors.

Historians believe that the medical care of northern and southern soldiers was similar. But records from the war are incomplete and sometimes inaccurate. Statistics in this book are current estimates.

Few official Confederate medical records survived the war. When the Rebel government evacuated its capital, Richmond, Virginia, in April 1865, out-of-control fires destroyed the office of the southern army's surgeon general, where these records had been stored.

Richmond's ruins, April 1865

After the war, the U.S. government published the multivolume *Medical and Surgical History of the War of the Rebellion*. Besides the North's medical records, the history incorporated information collected from surviving records of southern hospitals and individual Confederate surgeons.

Thousands of photographs of Civil War scenes were taken by northern photographers, particularly those working for Mathew Brady. Many have been preserved. Photographs from the South are rarer. *Blood and Germs*, therefore, contains more images depicting Union activities than Confederate. Most of the individual medical photographs and cases in this book involve Union soldiers in U.S. Army hospitals. The Confederate soldiers who appear in these photographs were prisoners.

A note on terms:

Military doctors were called *surgeons*, even though they didn't all perform surgery.

Soldiers of the United States Army (the North, or the Union) were called *Federals* or *Yankees*. Soldiers of the Confederate States of America Army (the South, or the Confederates) were called *Rebels*.

Both armies were divided into groups stationed in different regions of the country. For example, the Union's Army of the Potomac and the Confederate's Army of Northern Virginia fought in the eastern states.

When soldiers enlisted, they joined a *regiment* of about 1,000 men. The initial size varied, and it decreased as men left because of injury, illness, or death. Regiments were part of larger groups within the armies, such as brigades and divisions.

The North and South had different names for some of the battles. To avoid confusion, the first time I refer to any of these, I indicate both names. Subsequently, I use only the North's name, which is more common today.

A Currier & Ives print depicts the Battle of Fair Oaks (the North's name)/Seven Pines (the South's name), fought May 31 and June 1, 1862, in Virginia. During the nineteenth century, a New York company owned by Nathaniel Currier and James Merritt Ives published popular prints like this one. Scenes were created after the event and weren't necessarily accurate.

A Confederate (left) and Union soldier pose with their muskets.

CHAPTER ONE

"A DAY OF WAR AND BLOODSHED"

> "There is many a boy here today who looks on war as all glory, but, boys, it is all hell."
> —WILLIAM TECUMSEH SHERMAN, UNION GENERAL

As a bright sun rose on July 21, 1861, the soldiers knew the day would be sweltering. The war was just three months old, and most of the men had never been in battle before. They couldn't imagine the shocking carnage they were about to see.

The stakes were high that Sunday morning as tens of thousands of Americans faced each other in the Virginia countryside. The Federal army was there to preserve the union of the United States. For the Confederates, the independence of the eleven seceding southern states was on the line. In the words of a Confederate general: "Defeat to either side would be a deep mortification."

During previous days, Union troops had marched nearly thirty miles from Washington toward Manassas, a railroad junction strategically important to the Confederates. Northerners anticipated a glorious victory that would put the South in its place and end the rebellion. Curious Washington men and women, reporters, and members of Congress were eager to

watch a thrilling battle. On that hot morning, they packed picnic baskets and drove out from the city in carriages.

Confederate troops waited confidently for the Union army along a stream called Bull Run. Many in the South expected their foe to give up the fight against secession once the first northern blood was spilled.

At 5:30 that morning, the North's artillery guns fired, and the battle began. Soon the air was thick with dust and smoke and lead.

The booming roar of cannons was deafening. "Shell after shell burst above us," remembered a Confederate soldier, "ball after ball burst whizzing through the air." For a Union soldier, all other sounds were drowned out by "the thunder of artillery, the clash of steel, and the continuous roar of musketry."

Bullets and artillery shells shredded trees and ripped through human bodies. Men collapsed in agony. Their blood turned the ground deep red.

"The sight of falling men, wounded and killed," recalled an eighteen-year-old Confederate volunteer, "was more terrible than any words can describe; it froze the blood in our veins."

The scene was no less gruesome for the Federals. "I remember with what horror I saw the first man fall, killed instantly by a cannon shot," a Massachusetts soldier said, "and our men passed over him, trampling him in the dirt."

The battle raged on in the scorching heat. Troops on both sides were exhausted and thirsty.

A twenty-four-year-old Virginian dodged bullets as he cared for injured Rebels. "I witnessed the oft described horror of a battle field. Men lying in every nook and corner, wounded dying and dead."

A Union soldier was haunted by the same grisly sights. "Men tossing their arms wildly calling for help; there they lie bleeding, torn and mangled; legs, arms and bodies are crushed and broken as if smitten by thunder-bolts."

Army surgeons did what they could for the injured who made it to makeshift medical stations close to the fighting. In a church, a Union doctor bent over bleeding soldiers, bandaging wounds and performing amputations. "The men were lying upon every seat, between all the seats, and on every foot of the floor . . . My hands were stiff with blood."

One soldier's arm had been almost completely torn off at the shoulder by an artillery shot. Doctors realized "he was dying of the shock." They could do little for him.

By late afternoon, the Confederates had the upper hand. Union soldiers retreated, with thousands running in fear away from the Rebel guns. "The retreat then became a rout, soon degenerating into a panic," a northern magazine later reported. "So utterly demoralized were our forces that no attempt was made at a stand."

In the confusion, hundreds of injured Union men were left behind, helplessly lying on the ground with gaping wounds. Some would lie there for days until aid came. Others were captured by the Confederates.

Any Federals still able to walk straggled back to Washington. Few wagons were left to carry them. At the first sound of gunfire that morning, the civilian ambulance drivers hired by the U.S. Army had turned their wagons around and fled.

Nearly 1,500 Union soldiers had been killed or wounded. More than 1,300 were missing or captured. The astounding loss, observed one reporter, "cast a gloom over the remnants of the Army, and excited the deepest melancholy throughout Washington."

The city's temporary hospitals in hotels and government buildings were poorly managed and lacked medical supplies. They couldn't handle the shattered bodies that flooded the city. The U.S. Army's medical department

An illustration, published in *Harper's Weekly* magazine nearly three weeks after the battle, shows Union and Confederate soldiers retrieving the wounded. The image didn't tell the whole story. Because the Union army was forced to retreat, many of their wounded lay on the battlefield for several days until ambulances arrived to transport them to Washington.

hadn't bothered setting up a military hospital system. Officials expected only a ninety-day war with limited casualties.

In the South, newspapers announced "a decisive victory" at Manassas. Yet close to 2,000 Confederates had been killed or wounded. Hundreds of the most badly injured were taken by slow freight trains to Virginia towns and to the southern capital, Richmond, more than a hundred miles away. These communities, like Washington, were unprepared for such bloodshed. Private homes, factories, barns, and churches had to be turned into hospitals.

This deadly battle—called Bull Run by the North and Manassas by the South—was the first major clash of the American Civil War. Far bloodier battles would follow.

But the violence of the battlefield wasn't the greatest danger that soldiers faced. Disease killed twice as many men as did the bullets and artillery shells. Pneumonia, diarrhea, tuberculosis, measles, and smallpox were just some of the afflictions that claimed the lives of at least 400,000 men.

Because military records from the time are inexact and incomplete, historians disagree about the total number of Civil War deaths. Estimates range between 620,000 and 750,000 men. Even the lowest number is greater than all American deaths by battle wounds and disease in almost two hundred years of U.S. wars from the Revolutionary War through the Korean Conflict.

These deaths amounted to more than 2 percent of the United States population. Today, that would be as if all the residents of the cities of Los Angeles and Chicago — about 7 million people — perished during a four-year period.

Of those who survived the Civil War, hundreds of thousands suffered from chronic illnesses and painful, disabling wounds that plagued them long after the war ended. As many as 45,000 men had lost an arm or leg to amputation. For veterans whose bodies had been racked by sickness and injury, death often came well before they reached old age.

The Civil War continued until spring 1865. Its four tragic years of blood and germs would be a medical fiasco for the nation.

An 1889 lithograph memorializes the Battle of Bull Run. It depicts Union soldiers in blue and Confederates in gray. Actually, at this stage in the war, neither army had a standard uniform. This created confusion during battle when soldiers couldn't tell friend from foe. The men in red pants are wearing a Zouave uniform chosen by their Union regiment to imitate the French Zouave soldiers, admired for their bravery and fighting ability.

The Confederate flag flies over Fort Sumter in Charleston, South Carolina, three days after the Rebels' bombardment started the Civil War.

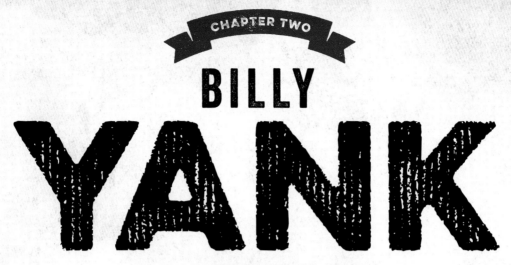

CHAPTER TWO

BILLY YANK
AND
JOHNNY REB

> "The spirit of these men was willing,
> but the flesh was weak."
> —W. S. KING, UNION SURGEON

Like most wars, this one didn't begin overnight. Tensions between the North and South had been brewing for decades as the two sides argued over the issue of slavery. Some lawmakers and citizens worked hard to avoid armed conflict. Others on both sides welcomed a military fight to settle differences between the regions once and for all. Uneasy Americans waited for the inevitable spark that would ignite war.

SIGN UP!

The last straw for Southerners was the November 1860 presidential election of Republican Abraham Lincoln, who opposed allowing slavery in the new western territories. South Carolina announced it was breaking away from the United States. Eventually, ten more southern slave states seceded, forming the Confederate States of America.

On April 12, 1861, Confederate cannons in Charleston, South Carolina, fired on the federal garrison at Fort Sumter in the harbor. The inferno of war had been lit.

Three days later, President Abraham Lincoln called for 75,000 volunteer soldiers. Each northern state was to recruit men from among its citizens to serve for three months. The existing U.S. Army had only 16,000 soldiers, not enough to end the rebellion. The Confederate ranks already included 60,000 soldiers, who had begun signing up as each southern state seceded.

Newspapers and politicians' speeches stoked patriotic emotions. Men rushed to enlist.

"Thousands of boys like me," a New Yorker wrote, "felt a sense of duty to aid the Union cause for service in the Army."

"No one stopped to reason and no one suggested failure," recalled one Virginian.

Most people didn't expect the war to last more than a few months. Each side misjudged the determination and strength of the other. By the time the Civil War ended, about 4 million Americans had entered the conflict.

PASSING MUSTER

Before a man could become a Union or Confederate soldier, he had to pass an official medical examination. Recruitment doctors were supposed to check each volunteer, without his clothes, to ensure that his body was healthy and fit enough to be a soldier. But the medical exams were often performed quickly and superficially. In fact, several hundred women passed, even though both armies banned women from serving as soldiers.

WOMAN SOLDIERS

Sarah Emma Edmonds pretending to be Franklin Thompson

SARAH EMMA

Sarah Emma Edmonds was one of the women who managed to pass the lax enlistment physical exam. She concealed her gender so that she could serve as a Union soldier named Franklin Thompson.

No one knows exactly how many women served as Civil War soldiers. Estimates range from 400 to 750. Some females enlisted so that they could be with brothers or husbands. Others were on their own, determined to fight for a cause they believed in. Edmonds later said: "I could only thank God that I was free and could go forward and work, and was not obliged to stay at home and weep."

With a short haircut, tightly bound breasts, and loose clothes, a young woman was able to blend in with the teenage boys in the ranks. But it was challenging to keep the secret while living in close quarters with men. If a woman was found out, the army usually sent her home. Impostors were occasionally discovered when they became ill or wounded and required medical care. Those who pulled off the deception spent the war fighting battles, acting as nurses and cooks, and even spying on the enemy. A few were taken as prisoners.

Edmonds joined a Michigan infantry in May 1861 at age nineteen. Serving as a stretcher bearer and hospital attendant, she accompanied her regiment to battles at Bull Run in 1861, and Antietam/Sharpsburg, Maryland, and Fredericksburg, Virginia, in 1862. In April 1863, she developed a high fever from malaria. Knowing that she wouldn't be able to hide her gender in a military hospital, Edmonds deserted and went to a private hospital as a woman. Upon recovering from her illness months later, she returned to the Union army as a female volunteer nurse.

After the war, Edmonds wrote a book about her experiences, including her daring exploits as a spy. Historians think she embellished her story. But her writings still provide insight into the life of a female soldier.

Edmonds married and raised three children. In 1886, the federal government acknowledged her service as Franklin Thompson and granted her a pension. She died in 1898.

Frances Hook in a photograph labeled Frank Henderson, one of her aliases

FRANCES

Posing as a young man named Frank, fourteen-year-old orphan Frances Hook followed her brother when he joined an Illinois regiment in April 1861. After he was killed in battle a year later, Frances enlisted in another regiment using a different last name. During the next two years, "Frank" was wounded twice and captured by the Confederates. Each time, her gender was discovered. Each time, she was sent home. Each time, Frances reenlisted under a new alias, because she was alone and had nowhere else to go. After the war, Frances married and had at least one child.

BROTHERS
GO TO
WAR

THE ELLSWORTHS OF NEW HAMPSHIRE

The Moore brothers of Virginia

The Ellsworth brothers of New Hampshire

The Ellsworth brothers, from Wentworth, New Hampshire, enlisted as privates in the Union army at the end of August 1862. Twins Bartlett and John were thirty-nine, and Samuel was forty-two.

Although they were hardy farmers, the Ellsworths were older than the majority of volunteers. The war took a toll on them. Bartlett died of typhoid fever in December 1862 at a camp near Fredericksburg. A few months later at the May 1863 Battle of Chancellorsville, Virginia, nearly half of the Ellsworths' regiment was killed or wounded. Samuel was captured and released after about two weeks. In October 1864, he deserted the army. In September 1864, John was discharged with an unspecified disability.

Several other Ellsworths from Wentworth—possibly relatives—joined the New Hampshire regiment at the same time as the three brothers. Benjamin, age forty-two, was wounded and discharged seven months later. Thomas, twenty-four, was killed at Chancellorsville. Jason, in his early thirties, died of typhoid fever in a Union hospital in June 1863. George, who enlisted at age eighteen, died of his wounds at the Battle of Cold Harbor, Virginia, in June 1864. In the same battle, James was wounded, but the twenty-four-year-old recovered and served until the end of the war.

THE MOORES OF VIRGINIA

In spring 1862, as the South anticipated an attack on the Moores' home city of Richmond, John and William enlisted in the Confederate army. They were only sixteen. The boys' older brother had joined the year before, at age eighteen, but their mother did not give her consent for the younger boys. She sent a letter to the surgeon of their regiment, attaching a note from the family's doctor stating that John and William were too sickly to serve in the army. Their true age revealed, the boys were sent home.

William enlisted again when he was eighteen. While seeing action during nine months of fighting, he rose through the ranks from private to captain. In 1865, William was wounded in battle at Petersburg, Virginia, and taken prisoner. The war in Virginia ended a week later, and William was released. He lived to be sixty.

The minimum age for army enlistment was eighteen, when males were considered full grown and sufficiently strong. Although eight in ten Civil War soldiers were between ages eighteen and twenty-nine, the armies accepted men who were as old as seventy and suffered from debilitating ailments. Most volunteers older than forty proved to be too unfit to withstand the stress of marching long distances, carrying heavy loads, sleeping on the ground, and fighting.

In spring 1862, the Union army's medical director reported that his forces had become a dumping ground for "the aged and infirm, the blind, the lame, and the deaf." Officials tried to clamp down on the loose enlistment examinations. They threatened fines or prison for doctors who allowed physically unqualified men to enlist. Examiners were told to reject volunteers suffering from insanity, cancer, deafness, a paralyzed leg or arm, or lack of a hand or foot.

Still, the standards remained low. The minimum height for northern enlistees was five feet, three inches, but this rule was frequently ignored. A man could be blind in one eye, as long as he could aim a gun with the other. He needed only enough teeth to tear open a paper cartridge, which held gunpowder and a bullet. He could be missing fingers, though he had to be able to pull a trigger. An enlistee was required to have his big toes so that he could manage the long marches.

As the war went on, Southerners felt outnumbered by the Yankees. Drawing from a smaller population than the Union, the Confederate army became desperate for soldiers. "We have come to the end of our tether," said one woman, "except we wait for the yearly crop of boys as they grow up to the requisite age."

New rules forced men between seventeen and fifty to serve, overlooking defects such as heart trouble and epilepsy. "All were accepted, sick or well, half blind, deaf or crippled—it mattered not, they were enrolled at once," wrote one southern soldier. By 1864, the last year of the war, the Confederate army had to obtain its soldiers "by robbing the cradle and the grave—the men too old, the boys too young."

CHILDREN ALLOWED

Young boys below the minimum enlistment age yearned to experience the glory and adventure of war. They lied about their age in order to be accepted as soldiers. Recruiters, with quotas to fill, were happy to believe them. Historians estimate that hundreds of thousands of boys seventeen and younger enlisted, including hundreds who were thirteen and under.

One way the Union and Confederate armies were officially willing to take young boys was as buglers or drummers. The boys' job was to announce roll call, sick call, drills, and marches to battle. They also performed camp chores such as gathering wood and running errands for officers. Some helped move wounded soldiers off the battlefield.

Johnny Cook, a fifteen-year-old bugler from Ohio, stepped in at the Battle of Antietam during a Confederate attack on his artillery unit. Rebel bullets had wounded or killed most of the soldiers who manned the Union cannons. Johnny grabbed a pouch of ammunition from a dead man and helped fire the weapons. For his bravery, he was awarded the Congressional Medal of Honor after the war.

Cook survived Antietam. But thirteen-year-old drummer Charlie King, from Pennsylvania, wasn't as lucky. He was killed by an exploding artillery shell.

Despite the courage displayed by some boys, many officers weren't happy to have the young drummers and buglers around. One Union doctor complained that they were "a perfect nuisance" because most couldn't drum or bugle, didn't show up for battles, and didn't do their work in camp.

As Union and Confederate leaders soon discovered, their volunteer armies weren't physically ready for war. Before fighting a single battle, thousands of soldiers had to be discharged for incapacitating ailments they'd had when they enlisted.

But removing the weakest recruits wasn't enough. Neither the armies nor the soldiers were prepared for the war's greatest threat. Disease.

DRUMMERS AND BUGLERS

Johnny Clem, age twelve, in 1863. He lived until 1937.

Johnny Clem was only ten when he unofficially joined a Michigan regiment as a drummer boy. After two years, he was allowed to enlist and be paid as a drummer. At the Battle of Chickamauga, Georgia, in September 1863, the twelve-year-old reportedly shot and killed a Rebel colonel who tried to take him prisoner. Northern newspapers made Johnny famous as the brave "Drummer-Boy of Chickamauga."

Clem was wounded two times before being discharged from the army at age thirteen. After the war, he finished high school and, in 1871, President Ulysses Grant appointed him as a second lieutenant. Clem remained in the U.S. Army until 1915 and officially retired as a major general.

This drummer boy, identified as Taylor, was a member of a U.S. Colored Troops regiment.

A young Union bugler poses with his instrument.

Union drummer boys play cards with older soldiers outside a winter shelter in 1862.

CHAPTER THREE

BUGS, PARASITES, AND MICROBES

> "Where balls have destroyed hundreds, insidious diseases, with their long train of symptoms, and quiet, noiseless progress, sweep away thousands."
>
> —J. JULIAN CHISOLM, CONFEDERATE SURGEON

Nineteen-year-old Harvey Wiley had never been more than twenty miles from his family's Indiana farm. In July 1864, he found himself based in Tennessee with the regiment he had recently joined.

After just two months living in the Union camp, the young man fell ill with what he thought was a bad cold. But soon, he was burning with fever and covered with a red rash. The regiment's doctor diagnosed measles. Even after the spots disappeared within a few days, the soldier was left with a severe cough. Several weeks passed before Wiley had the stamina to carry out his full duties.

THE HIDDEN ENEMY

Bullets and cannonballs were obvious threats to life. But the armies' medical departments recognized the significant danger of sickness among the troops. The Confederate *Manual of Military Surgery*, distributed to its army doctors, reinforced this concern. "Disease is the fell destroyer of armies, and stalks at all times through encampments," it warned. "To keep an army in health is, then, even more important than to cure wounds from the battle-fields."

Keeping the armies healthy proved to be a challenge. In 1861, doctors were familiar with measles, mumps, and smallpox. They realized that the sick frequently passed their illnesses on to others. Yet because of careless medical exams during the rush to build up the forces, recruits were allowed to join when they had these contagious diseases. Tens of thousands of new soldiers flocked to military camps. It didn't take long for epidemics to break out.

Army doctors had expected the volunteers from rural areas to be stronger and healthier than the city recruits. Men who worked on farms made up nearly half the Union army and an even higher proportion of the Confederate army. But despite being used to hard physical work and developing strong muscles, the farm workers fell ill more often. A major reason was that they had spent their lives in small, isolated communities.

Soldiers relax at a Union camp. When many men lived in close quarters, diseases flourished.

They had never been exposed to the contagious diseases they encountered in army camps, and they lacked immunity to them.

No vaccines existed to prevent measles, mumps, influenza, or pneumonia. There were no antibiotics to fight infections such as tuberculosis. Germ theory was decades away, and doctors didn't know that microbes caused these diseases. As a result, a Civil War soldier was twice as likely to die of disease than from a battle wound.

RED SPOTS AND SWOLLEN FACES

Measles and mumps were two diseases usually contracted during childhood, providing lifelong immunity. The soldiers who hadn't been exposed to either one were susceptible.

Measles is so contagious that one sick person will infect nine of ten people with whom he or she has contact. When someone carrying the measles virus sneezes, coughs, or simply breathes, he sends microbes into the air and onto surfaces. Others are infected by inhaling the virus or by transferring it to their mouth, eyes, or nose after touching a contaminated surface.

A measles infection lasts about three weeks unless the patient has complications, such as bronchitis or pneumonia. In those serious cases, recovery can take months. For some soldiers, measles was deadly. In the Union army, more than 76,000 soldiers came down with the disease. About 7 percent died.

During the summer of 1861, measles swept through the camps of new recruits. One in seven Confederate soldiers stationed in Northern Virginia developed the disease. In a few newly formed Confederate regiments, measles "proved so fatal in camp that companies, battalions and whole regiments had to be disbanded for a time and the men sent home."

Like measles, mumps is caused by a virus that spreads from person to person through saliva. The infection strikes salivary glands on the side of the face, making them swell and hurt. An infected person runs a fever, feels achy, and has no energy. During the Civil War, about 60,000 Union soldiers developed mumps, though fewer than 100 died.

Most soldiers recovered from a bout of measles or mumps, but they often felt weak and ill for several weeks. These men weren't able to fight. Military leaders couldn't carry out battle plans when large numbers of their troops were sick.

DREADED SMALLPOX

Smallpox is caused by a virus. Victims develop high fevers, body aches, and fluid-filled skin sores. The blisters scab over and leave a scar. With no cure, smallpox killed more than a third of its victims during epidemics. Survivors sometimes were blind, but they were protected from reinfection.

The smallpox virus is transmitted by infected droplets in a victim's sneeze, cough, or breath. It can even spread on contaminated bedding and clothing. Because it is so contagious, military doctors feared outbreaks.

Vaccination against smallpox had been practiced in America for more than one hundred years. A bit of scab or fluid from a smallpox sore was introduced into a person's body through a cut in the skin. He or she developed a mild case of the disease and immunity to future infection.

MEASLES

In early March 1863, Private George Foster, age nineteen, broke out in spots while in camp with his Michigan regiment outside Washington. Instead of recovering as most measles patients did, Foster deteriorated. When he developed pneumonia, the regiment's doctor sent him by wagon to the nearby Union hospital in Alexandria, Virginia. By then, Foster was feverish and delirious. His breathing became labored, and he coughed up blood. The young soldier steadily grew worse. Four days after arriving at the hospital, he died, one of about 5,000 fatal measles cases in the Union army.

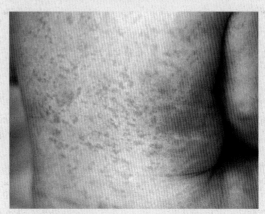

The red measles spots on a child's back. Other symptoms are fever, runny nose, and cough. Victims may develop pneumonia, and some will die.

In 1798, English scientist Edward Jenner publicized his use of a safer vaccine using cowpox pus or scabs. Cowpox, found in cows and calves, was similar enough to smallpox to provide immunity without causing the more dangerous human disease.

At the time of the Civil War, vaccination was usually done using a scab from a cowpox sore or from a previously vaccinated person. The doctor cut the recipient's skin, normally on the upper arm. Then he inserted the inoculating material into the cut. If the smallpox vaccine worked, the area developed a sore, scabbed over, and left a scar. The vaccinated person now had immunity to the disease.

People living in American cities often were vaccinated, typically as children. Vaccination was rare in rural areas of the North and South because smallpox outbreaks there were less common. The majority of soldiers had never been vaccinated.

When smallpox cases showed up, medical departments of both armies acted to head off an epidemic. They isolated sick men in hospital tents or buildings, called pest houses. Bedding and clothes belonging to the infected patients were destroyed.

To stop the disease's spread, army surgeons ordered vaccinations for soldiers and new recruits who lacked a vaccine scar. Doctors eventually noticed that even those with the scar could get smallpox. The vaccine apparently didn't offer lifelong protection. The armies required revaccination for anyone who hadn't been inoculated within the previous seven years. Unfortunately, the individual states didn't follow these guidelines when enlisting soldiers, and not all Civil War troops were protected.

According to records from the Union medical department, close to 19,000 soldiers in the U.S. Army developed smallpox, and 7,000 of them died. No exact count exists for

SMALLPOX

Private Saul Millhollin worked as a cook for his Minnesota regiment. One day in early December 1862, he suddenly developed a headache and fever. Two days later, Millhollin felt severe pain in his back. Ugly red sores erupted on his hands and face. Doctors at a Union hospital diagnosed smallpox.

During the next several days, the sores completely covered Milhollin's body. Swallowing was painful. Doctors gave him an opium-based drug for his pain. They also tried quinine and various other medicines to ease his discomfort. It was no use. Two weeks after he first fell ill, Millhollin fainted while using the toilet. Within a half hour, he was dead.

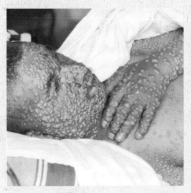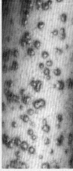

This man (left) is covered by smallpox sores. A victim's arm (right) shows the red blisters. These photographs were taken in the first half of the twentieth century. Thanks to more effective vaccines and a worldwide vaccination program, smallpox is now considered eradicated.

the Confederates, but the southern army experienced similar outbreaks.

Historians believe that smallpox struck President Abraham Lincoln in November 1863, at the time he gave the Gettysburg Address in Pennsylvania. His recovery took about a month.

INFECTED LUNGS

Life in the military was hard on the body, especially during bad weather. Soldiers often slept on the wet, cold ground with only a blanket to keep warm. A Union soldier camped outside of Washington in January 1862 wrote: "We are dying faster from the sicknesses of camp than from the casualties of war. Nearly all the men have bad colds, so that sometimes during a concert the coughing fairly drowns the music. . . . Where the rebels kill one, disease slays ten."

Rebel soldiers from the Deep South weren't used to the freezing winters and snow farther north. After the Confederacy began to run out of money, adequate clothing and blankets were in short supply. By early 1863, one brigade of 1,500 soldiers in the Army of Northern Virginia had 400 men with no shoes and many with no coats.

These conditions made the men susceptible to colds and influenza, caused by viruses, which spread among soldiers living in small tents and crowded buildings. The illnesses often progressed to the lung infections bronchitis and pneumonia. Without antibiotics, a sick person recovered only if his immune system fought off the infection. This was more difficult when the patient was weakened by lack of rest, nutritious food, and warmth.

During 1862 and 1863, Confederate doctors reported that one in six southern soldiers had pneumonia. Union medical records show that about 20,000 soldiers died of pneumonia, making it one of the war's top killer diseases.

Tuberculosis, also called consumption, is a lung disease caused by bacteria. The disease made its victims too weak to endure military life, and recruitment doctors were supposed to reject any man with tuberculosis symptoms. Many ended up in the armies anyway, later being sent home to recover or dying in army hospitals.

The tuberculosis patient has a bad cough, often bringing up blood. Other symptoms include chest pain, fever, weakness, and weight loss. The bacteria spread by coughs and sneezes. Unaware of the disease's cause and transmission, Civil War doctors didn't isolate a sick patient.

They treated tuberculosis by trying to strengthen the victim's body so that it healed itself. A patient was given cod-liver oil, warm clothes, exercise, plenty of food, and alcohol. In the 1860s, physicians considered alcoholic beverages like whiskey, beer, and wine to be stimulants that helped a patient rally. Actually, such drinks are depressants, the opposite. Tuberculosis patients also received quinine to lower their fever and opium or morphine to ease their coughs.

Because there was no effective treatment, the illness could be a long one and frequently ended with death. Today, doctors treat tuberculosis with antibiotics. These medicines did not exist in the 1860s.

TUBERCULOSIS

Daniel Burdickson, nineteen, was a private in a U.S. Colored Troops regiment from Indiana. In early December 1864, he was admitted with tuberculosis to a Union hospital for black soldiers in Alexandria, Virginia. Burdickson was weak and slept most of the time. After a month at the hospital, his cough had gotten much worse, producing thick mucus that sometimes contained blood. Doctors could do nothing for him. He languished for nearly two more weeks before dying. The next day, Burdickson was buried in Soldiers' Cemetery, now called the Alexandria National Cemetery.

Many of the black Union soldiers, especially former slaves, were susceptible to disease because they came from rural areas. They had never been exposed to illnesses such as measles and smallpox, and they had no immunity. Some former slaves suffered from malnutrition when they enlisted. The body of any malnourished recruit was less able to resist infections encountered in the crowded military camps.

TOXIC SWAMPS

Soldiers who served in the U.S. Army before the war knew that illnesses were more common in certain environments. Experienced officers avoided setting up camps near low, swampy areas because the men often developed malaria. This disease weakens its victim, creating chills, sweating, and high fever. Once infected, a person can suffer the symptoms on and off for years.

In the 1860s, physicians and scientists believed that miasma—poisonous air from rotting plant or animal material—carried disease. If something gave off a foul smell, such as a swamp or standing water, it brought on sicknesses like malaria.

Doctors didn't know that the disease is caused by a parasite transmitted by *Anopheles* mosquitoes. After an infected mosquito bites a person, the parasites invade the body's bloodstream and organs, causing malaria symptoms. Malaria occurs in wet, warm areas because mosquitoes breed under those conditions.

Civil War doctors hadn't connected mosquito bites to malaria, but they did have a treatment. Quinine, made from the bark of the South American cinchona tree, effectively reduced symptoms and helped to prevent the disease.

When soldiers were stationed near swampy areas, they swallowed a ration of quinine each day, often mixed with whiskey to mask the strong taste. After the North blockaded shipping into southern ports, the Confederates had trouble getting quinine. They smuggled it in or stole it from captured Union troops. Though they tried to make a similar drug from local tree barks, the effort failed.

Malaria sickened soldiers on both sides, affecting more men than any diseases other than diarrhea and dysentery. At least a million Union soldiers suffered from it. The numbers are thought to have been even higher among the Confederates, partly because they couldn't get enough quinine. Although malaria didn't kill many soldiers, it could incapacitate an army and force changes in battle plans.

Mosquitoes were also behind outbreaks of yellow fever. The disease is caused by a virus carried by the female *Aedes aegypti* mosquito. This mosquito can't survive cold temperatures, and the illness was most common in the South. Early symptoms include fever, headache, vomiting, and yellow complexion. No special treatment cured it, and the disease was often fatal. Fortunately, yellow fever epidemics during the war were small and limited to coastal areas in North and South Carolina and at Key West, Florida.

THE BIG ITCH

Soldiers had plenty of mosquitoes, miserable weather, and muddy marches. What they lacked was soap. Both Yankees and Rebels complained about the shortages. With many unwashed human bodies in filthy clothes living in close contact, body lice became a widespread curse.

One Rebel described an infestation by the graybacks, whose "crawling made his flesh creep; their attacks inflamed his blood and skin." Despite soldiers' efforts to pick off the biting insects or boil their clothes, "these pests skirmished around as usual, though where they came from or how they arrived were mysteries we never solved."

The lice laid their eggs in seams of the uniforms, and it was nearly impossible to get them out. Soldiers made the best of the situation, amusing themselves by betting on louse races staged on top of a metal plate.

Lice transmit typhus, which can be fatal. Yet even though most of the soldiers were infested at some point during the war, only about 2,600 cases of typhus were reported in the Union army. Medical historians believe the majority of those were actually typhoid fever, which has similar symptoms. Besides discomfort, the worst health impact of the lice was that they caused soldiers to scratch themselves, creating skin cuts that became infected.

Fleas and bedbugs were also a scourge in camps and hospitals. A Union army nurse wrote of her battle with insects when she was stationed on the North Carolina coast in spring 1865. "The other day I could not stand it a moment longer, rushed into my room and went hunting; the result was thirty fleas, the biggest louse you ever saw, and in the covering of my hoopskirt an enormous bedbug had built her nest and laid her eggs."

As annoying as the bugs were, far more perilous threats lurked in a gulp of water or a trip to the latrine.

U.S. soldiers fighting in France during World War I pick body lice from the seams of their clothing just as Civil War soldiers had done fifty years before.

A microscopic view of a body louse. The dark spot in its abdomen is blood ingested when it bit a human.

A woman and her children pose with members of a Pennsylvania regiment camped outside Washington in 1862. She holds a basket of laundry. Some soldiers brought their families to war. The women cooked and did laundry for their husbands and other soldiers. At times, they helped nurse the sick.

THE VIRGINIA QUICKSTEP

> "We have a great deal of sickness
> among the soldiers, and now
> those on the sick-list would form an army."
> —ROBERT E. LEE, CONFEDERATE GENERAL

Private Edgar Sanborn, fifteen, enlisted in the Union army in New Hampshire. During the Siege of Petersburg, Virginia, in the summer of 1864, he fell ill. His body was hot with fever. He had diarrhea and abdominal pain. His pulse was weak. The camp doctors diagnosed typhoid fever and sent Sanborn to a military hospital in Washington for care. It was too late. He was barely conscious, and within a week of reaching the hospital, the teen had died.

FILTH AND STENCH

People smelled the camps before they saw them. Soldiers went weeks without washing their bodies or their clothes. Although U.S. Army regulations called for bathing once a week, that rarely happened.

An even more offensive odor came from the latrine pits full of urine and feces.

Medical departments of both armies had regulations to maintain camp hygiene and to reduce the chance of disease. The Confederate *Manual of Military Surgery* reminded its doctors: "Cleanliness of the encampment, of the tent, and also of the body and clothing of soldiers, should never be forgotten."

The regulations called for latrines to be dug in long trenches at least five feet deep. Poles or boards with holes were to be laid over the sewage pits so that soldiers could sit on them to relieve their bowels. Each day, dirt was to be thrown over the accumulated urine and feces. When the pit was less than two feet from the top, a new latrine should be dug.

But the armies were made up of state regiments manned with officers and doctors who lacked experience in keeping camps healthy. They often didn't enforce the rules. The pits were too shallow, and they weren't covered daily. The latrines overflowed. Because of the nauseating smell, many men avoided using them. Instead, soldiers relieved themselves in the nearby fields and woods. That only added to the camp stink.

Physicians blamed contaminated air for illnesses and infections among the soldiers. One Union doctor pointed the finger at camp miasma: "The air is poisoned by putrid exhalations from the liquid discharges of diarrhoea, dysentery, and fever cases."

He and everyone else were wrong about the miasma, but they were right that the camp stench was a sign of conditions making soldiers sick. Human waste full of disease-causing bacteria polluted the food and drinking water.

Because no one understood that, people didn't worry about washing hands after urinating and defecating and before touching food. When they scooped drinking water from dirty streams and runoff, they didn't boil it, which would have killed the dangerous microbes. As a result, diarrhea, dysentery, and typhoid fever became common diseases among the soldiers.

THE RUNS

Nearly every soldier had at least one bout of diarrhea or dysentery. Diarrhea symptoms included watery feces and the frequent need to defecate. The ailment could last a few days or as long as weeks or months. For those

DIARRHEA

PRISONER OF THE YANKEES

Confederate Alexander Stowe, age twenty-eight, was captured from his North Carolina regiment and taken to a prison camp. In October 1863, he became so sick with chronic diarrhea that he was sent to a Union hospital in Maryland. Doctors treated him with opium and whiskey.

Over the next month, Stowe seemed to improve. Then the diarrhea returned with new pain in the abdomen. Doctors prescribed quinine, turpentine, and an opium mixture. In late January, although still weak, Stowe climbed out of bed to walk around the hospital ward . . . and fell, dead.

During the war, army surgeons did autopsies on some soldiers who had died of illness or wounds, usually within twenty-four hours of death. The purpose was to learn more about diseases and injuries and to find out why they were fatal. Reports of the postmortems were sent to the U.S. Army medical department so that results could be shared with other surgeons.

A Union doctor performed an autopsy on Stowe, but "nothing was found in the organs to explain the cause of death."

PRISONER OF THE REBELS

Private Theodore Porter of Pennsylvania, age forty-seven, was held by the Confederate army as a prisoner of war for six months in 1863. During that time, he developed constant diarrhea. When Porter was released from the Richmond prison, Union doctors tried to heal him at a Maryland hospital.

But over several weeks, Porter's condition deteriorated until he was emaciated, and he was transferred to a larger military hospital in Philadelphia. There, doctors treated Porter with quinine, stimulants, iron, and nourishing food to strengthen him. They tried to stop the diarrhea with opium, laudanum, and calomel (made with mercury). Nothing worked. In late October 1863, less than two weeks after being admitted to the hospital, Porter began vomiting. In two days, he was dead.

who suffered for extended periods, their diarrhea led to dehydration, weakness, and extreme weight loss. These conditions could result in death. Chronic diarrhea killed more Civil War soldiers than any other disease.

Dysentery was similar, but it was more likely to cause death. Patients had fever, cramping, and bloody feces. Officers were concerned by these outbreaks because ill soldiers were less effective in battle.

Soldiers had several nicknames for the uncontrollable urge to empty their bowels. The name changed, depending on where their camp was located. Two favorites were the *Tennessee Trots* and the *Virginia Quickstep*. Men couldn't make it to the latrines in time, and they relieved their bowels near the tents. Not only did others inadvertently walk through the feces, but rain washed the waste into the creek or river that supplied the camp's drinking water.

Some soldiers never fully recovered from attacks of diarrhea or dysentery. Even after the war was over, the damage to their intestines and other organs remained, shortening their lives.

TYPHOID!

Typhoid fever victims suffered from diarrhea, too. Additional symptoms included high fever, red spots, and delirium. Among Civil War soldiers, typhoid was fatal in more than a third of cases, often because of bleeding from the intestine.

Doctors prescribed quinine, oil of turpentine, calomel, brandy, and opium. The medicines were ineffective. Without the antibiotics we have today to kill the typhoid bacteria, a patient's body had to fight the infection on its own. That took weeks or months. Survivors had immunity to reinfection.

Typhoid fever spreads when the bacteria leave the infected person's body in his feces. If someone ingests water or food contaminated by feces containing typhoid bacteria, he will be infected, too. With tens of thousands of troops camped in the same area, frequently along rivers, the water supply was soon polluted with body waste.

Food was contaminated when flies carried typhoid microbes from exposed feces in latrine pits to a soldier's meal. The disease could also spread if the cook was a typhoid victim and didn't wash his hands after using the latrine—a common behavior.

Besides sickening thousands of soldiers, typhoid attacked nurses who cared for ill soldiers in the army hospitals. Author Louisa May Alcott was one volunteer nurse who contracted the disease in a Washington hospital early in the war. She became so ill that she had to return home to Massachusetts.

Civilians were affected, too. In February 1862, President Abraham Lincoln's young son Willie died from typhoid fever.

TYPHOID FEVER

n December 1864, Private Edward Brown from Massachusetts was admitted to a Washington hospital with typhoid fever. The eighteen-year-old's skin was covered with rosy spots. Brown's abdomen was tender, and he was unable to control his bowels. Barely conscious, he muttered deliriously. Three days later, the teen was dead.

An autopsy was done on Brown's body. Symptoms of typhoid fever are similar to those of other diseases, and his doctor wanted to confirm that typhoid had killed him. During the autopsy, the doctor spotted the telltale sign of typhoid fever—damage to the lining of Brown's small intestine.

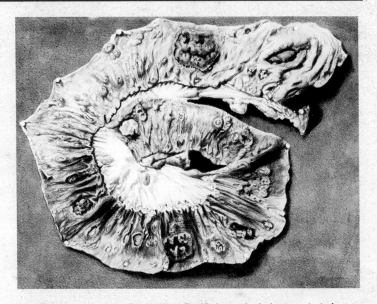

An 1859 photograph by Dr. William Budd shows the holes in a victim's small intestine caused by typhoid bacteria. In 1856, the British physician discovered that typhoid fever was transmitted by the feces of infected patients. To prevent this, Budd advised boiling polluted water before drinking. Unfortunately, his discovery was ignored by most of the American medical community. Instead, doctors and scientists blamed typhoid on miasma, fatigue, or exposure to harsh weather.

BAD FOOD

Some soldiers developed diarrhea after eating spoiled food. Without refrigeration, harmful bacteria multiplied and caused food poisoning. Foodborne illness was more prevalent during the warm summer months when food spoiled quickly.

Intestinal worms plagued soldiers, too. According to records kept by the Union's medical department, about 4,000 men became ill from parasitic worms that invaded their guts. In the 1860s, doctors didn't fully understand the connection between worms, sanitation, and disease.

Tapeworm infestation causes abdominal pain, diarrhea, weakness, and weight loss. Humans ingest tapeworms in undercooked meat containing tapeworm larvae or in water and food contaminated by feces containing tapeworm eggs. In 1864, a surgeon at a Maryland army hospital reported a soldier whose intestines harbored a twenty-foot tapeworm.

At the time, American scientists had not yet recognized infestations by the hookworm, an intestinal parasite found in the southeastern United

Cooks prepare a meal in a Union camp. Disease was rampant when hundreds of soldiers crowded together. Poor sanitation allowed intestinal bacteria from a sick man to spread to food and water, infecting others.

States. Hookworms enter the body through the mouth or skin, after the victim comes in contact with feces containing them. The parasites invade the intestines, causing weakness and anemia. Early in the 1900s, the American hookworm was identified and its symptoms described. Some former Civil War doctors believed that the parasite had, indeed, infected soldiers.

Only a handful of men died from parasite attacks. But the worms sapped their strength, making many soldiers more likely to die of other diseases or wounds.

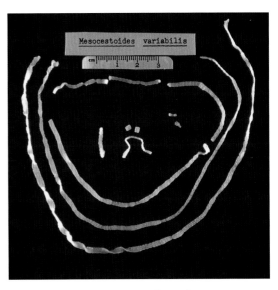

An entire tapeworm, broken in pieces, taken from a toddler's body in 1971.

BLEEDING GUMS

Eating spoiled or wormy food caused illnesses, but the *lack* of food was just as harmful. Malnourished men in both armies developed scurvy. Today we know that this disease occurs when the body doesn't get enough vitamin C, which is found in fresh fruit and vegetables.

Someone with scurvy feels fatigued. He might have bleeding gums, bleeding under the skin, achy joints, and diarrhea. Eventually, he could die from organ damage. Soldiers with scurvy became too weak to carry a knapsack, march, and fight. And because the body needs vitamin C to heal wounds, they suffered even more complications from their injuries.

Union doctors diagnosed at least 46,000 scurvy cases with nearly 800 deaths. But the symptoms can be vague at first, and there probably were many more undetected cases.

The discovery of vitamins and their effects on human health would not come for another fifty years. By the mid-nineteenth century, however, doctors had observed that fruits and vegetables prevented scurvy. Since the soldiers' regular diets of salted meat and bread lacked these foods, the Union army sometimes provided dried vegetables that the soldiers boiled in water. This didn't do much good, though. The heat destroyed any vitamin C the dried bits might have had.

SCURVY

I n early July 1863, Confederate private John Farthing from North Carolina was captured by the Union army during the Battle of Gettysburg. Later that month, the prisoner of war was admitted to a Union hospital in Harrisburg, Pennsylvania. He had swollen, bleeding gums. His pulse rate was weak, and his bowels were loose.

Union doctors diagnosed scurvy. They prescribed two lemons and a teaspoonful of lemon juice each day, as well as potassium iodide, opium pills, and camphor. In two weeks, Farthing had much improved. While the other drugs were given to treat his symptoms, the lemons—with high vitamin C content— healed his scurvy.

A medical book drawing of a man with scurvy. It shows bleeding under the skin and in the eyes as well as the listlessness of a scurvy victim.

In July 1862, a Union surgeon reported on conditions outside of Richmond after the U.S. Army had spent more than three months trying to capture the southern capital. "It is almost impossible to get anything to eat except beef and hard bread. Men are rotting with scurvy and have been for months, and no vegetables, and {the} government either cannot or will not furnish them."

Confederate general Robert E. Lee reported to the Rebel secretary of war in spring 1863 that "symptoms of scurvy are appearing among them, and to supply the place of vegetables each regiment is directed to send a daily detail to gather sassafras buds, wild onions, garlic, lamb's quarter, and poke sprouts." Soldiers also foraged for other edible green plants, including dandelions, and for berries and wild fruits.

As the war continued, food became scarcer for Confederate soldiers. Most battles were fought on southern soil, destroying farmland and reducing crop production. The Union blockades of the Mississippi River and ocean ports disrupted the South's importing of food from other countries. Transporting the available food to the troops by railroad was difficult. The Union army destroyed miles of tracks, and the Confederacy didn't have the materials to make repairs.

Southern soldiers were desperate for food. One wrote to his wife in summer 1862: "Whenever we stop for twenty-four hours every corn field and orchard within two or three miles is completely stripped."

After the August 1862 Second Battle of Bull Run in Virginia, a Confederate soldier noticed a difference between the Yankee and Rebel dead. He thought the bodies of Union soldiers had decayed and turned black, but Confederate bodies had not. In his opinion, the reason was clear: "The Federal troops were well cared for, well fed, fat, and in good physical condition; upon them decay and decomposition made quick work. The Confederates had little flesh upon them, no fat, nothing to decay."

Bad health could undermine an army, and commanders knew it. In August 1861, General J. Bankhead Magruder reported his concerns to Confederate headquarters. His troops on the Virginia Peninsula outside Richmond, he wrote, were suffering from typhoid fever, measles, malaria, and scurvy. One North Carolina regiment of 1,000 men had fewer than 400 fit for duty. Magruder implored the Confederate government to attend "promptly to the requisitions and suggestions of the medical officers as regards the sanitary condition of the troops."

SORE AND BROKEN

Even if a soldier managed to avoid disease, the grueling strain of army life could break his body. When troops were on the move, men often marched more than ten miles a day carrying thirty to fifty pounds of equipment, including a gun, ammunition, tent, blanket, and knapsack full of clothes and personal belongings.

Soldiers endured sunstroke and dehydration on hot days and exposure and hypothermia during cold rains and snow. Some of them suffered from back, shoulder, and knee pain. They also experienced nerve damage, torn muscles, and blisters that became infected.

INJURED

Private George Goundry, twenty-two, was born and raised in central New York. Upon enlisting in the Union army in January 1862, he was sent to a camp outside of Washington. After just two months, Goundry developed a sore on his left shoulder from carrying his gun and heavy knapsack. The infected area swelled and became painful, and he was sent to the regiment's hospital.

Despite six weeks of medical care, the abscess wouldn't heal. Because the injury left him unable to use his left arm, he was discharged from the army. Goundry's arm never returned to normal before his death fifty years later.

After marching more than twenty miles, a Vermont soldier described the ordeal: "If a man wants to know what it is to have every bone in his body ache with fatigue, every muscle sore and exhausted, and his whole body ready to sink to the ground, let him . . . shoulder his knapsack, haversack, gun and equipments, and make one of our forced marches."

HEARTACHE

Physical ailments weren't a soldier's only problems. Many struggled with nostalgia, a term used for extreme homesickness.

The typical soldier in his teens or early twenties had never been away from his family. In fact, he hadn't traveled farther than a few miles from the house where he was born. Suddenly, he was marched long miles from one strange battlefield to another, carrying a heavy knapsack and gun, feeling hungry, dripping wet, and either sweating or shivering. His only connection to home and loved ones was an occasional letter.

The military recognized that this "feeling of depression frequently pervaded our camps on account of discomfort, hardships and exposures." Affected soldiers often had no appetite, and they lost weight.

In March 1863, a Union surgeon reported to the army medical department that many of the men in his Illinois regiment, based in faraway Louisiana, suffered from nostalgia: "The state of the weather, their uncomfortable situation, the vast amount of sickness throughout the whole army and the numerous deaths—all combined to depress their spirits."

Some distraught men fled for home, willing to risk the punishment for desertion—death.

As the war dragged on, more and more soldiers on both sides became sick in body and soul. But they had not been forgotten by the people back home. Help was on the way.

DEADLY DISEASES

Disease killed about 400,000 men during the war. The count is based on official Union army medical department records and on estimates of Confederate victims. Record-keeping wasn't perfect, however, and the total might well have been higher.

Medical historians believe that southern troops suffered from the same illnesses as northern soldiers with roughly the same mortality rate. The number of deaths from the leading diseases in the Union army:

Diarrhea/dysentery: 44,500
Typhoid fever: 29,000
Pneumonia: 20,000
Smallpox: 7,000
Tuberculosis: 6,500
Malaria: 5,000

Nathaniel Shoup enlisted in a Pennsylvania infantry in October 1861. Less than nine months later, he was dead. After losing his battle with typhoid fever, Shoup was buried in the Alexandria [Virginia] National Cemetery. He was just eighteen or nineteen.

Confederate soldier Samuel Wilhelm served with a Virginia regiment. A father of six, Wilhelm was captured and taken to a Union prison in Delaware. Overcrowded with prisoners from the Battle of Gettysburg, Fort Delaware turned into a breeding ground for disease. In September 1863, Wilhelm's diarrhea killed him.

Joseph Judson Dimock, thirty-four, joined a New York infantry regiment as a major in May 1861. During the Virginia Peninsula Campaign, Dimock fell ill. He was one of thousands of soldiers who suffered from typhoid, dysentery, and malaria during the wet spring and summer of 1862. Standing water, overflowing creeks, and poor sanitation created perfect conditions for disease. On June 22, 1862, Dimock died from typhoid fever.

MERCURY AND MAGGOTS

At the time of the Civil War, no one knew what caused diseases. Doctors didn't have many real cures, such as antibiotics. They thought that a good diet and rest strengthened a sick person, allowing his body to restore itself to health. Some medicines and treatments intended to relieve symptoms and pain did more damage to the body than the illness.

The surgeon's most indispensable drugs were morphine and opium for pain, quinine for fever and pain, mercury for a variety of ailments, and ether and chloroform for anesthetizing patients during surgery.

The South had difficulty obtaining medicines. By most accounts, however, southern army doctors never ran out of ether or chloroform. The medical department tried to manufacture other drugs, with limited success. South Carolina doctor Francis Peyre Porcher wrote a book, *Resources of the Southern Fields and Forests*, that informed fellow Confederate surgeons of plants that could act as substitutes for the medicines in short supply. Few records remain to document how useful these plants were to military surgeons.

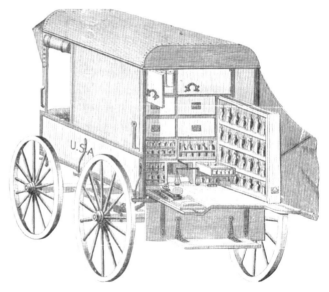

Specially equipped wagons followed the armies, transporting medical materials. This Union medicine wagon, called the Autenrieth, was introduced in 1864. Stored in the back were medicines, chloroform, surgical instruments, bandages, a stretcher, and blankets. Confederate troops celebrated when they were able to capture a Union medicine wagon and replenish their supplies.

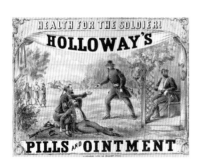

Many soldiers didn't trust the medicines dispensed by the military. Instead, they treated their ills with patent medicines sent from home or bought from sutlers (salesmen who followed the armies and sold goods from a wagon). The pills, tonics, and ointments didn't cure diseases. Many contained opium and alcohol, which numbed pain or put users to sleep. The company behind these advertisements aimed its products at Union soldiers. Drawings included Yankees in Zouave uniforms.

This military drug kit kept medicines organized and prevented bottles from breaking while regiments traveled.

OPIUM

Opium, made from poppies, successfully reduced pain and brought on sleep. Doctors also prescribed it for headaches, diarrhea, dysentery, and typhoid fever. The Union army used ten million opium pills and nearly one hundred tons of opium powder during the war. Some historians believe that soldiers sometimes became addicted to opium during their treatment.

MORPHINE

Derived from opium, morphine is ten times more powerful. Surgeons sprinkled it directly into a painful wound or injected a morphine solution using a syringe. Because the needles were not sharp, a small cut had to be made in the skin before the needle could be inserted. Doctors used the same syringes and needles over and over, probably spreading disease and infections.

MERCURY

Physicians turned to mercury to treat various ills. They gave soldiers blue mass (mercury mixed with licorice and a sweetener) or calomel (a mercury powder) as a laxative for constipation. Mercury was also an ingredient in ointments for skin diseases. The chemical accumulated in the body, and soldiers who swallowed too much suffered kidney damage, loose teeth, and deformed gums and jaw.

A Confederate surgeon described how he prescribed medicines to ill soldiers at the morning sick call: "In one pocket of my trousers I had a ball of blue mass [mercury], in another a ball of opium." He asked each man, "'How are your bowels?'" The doctor explained that if the soldier said they were loose, "I administered a plug of opium; if they were shut, I gave a plug of blue mass."

QUININE

Soldiers swallowed quinine to prevent and cure malaria, for which it was effective, and to reduce fevers, for which it was not. The South often had to rely on captured Union supplies, smugglers, or blockade runners to obtain quinine.

ALCOHOL

Today, alcoholic beverages are considered depressants. But during the war, they were used as stimulants to revive the sick and give them energy and strength.

TURPENTINE

Oil of turpentine was made from pine tree resin. Doctors prescribed it for typhoid fever and diarrhea, and as a tonic to kill intestinal worms. They soaked bandages in it to prevent infection and to keep insects from infesting wounds.

Flies were a constant pest in camps and hospitals. The insects were attracted to wounds, laying their eggs in them. The fly larvae, called maggots, ate the dead tissue of the wound without damaging healthy tissue. Although the wiggling maggots were itchy, they cleaned out the wound and prevented further infection. Some doctors and nurses saw the maggots' value. But most tried to kill the creatures using turpentine or camphor oil.

Maggots mixed with mud and leaves.

CHAPTER FIVE

ONIONS
FOR YOUR
SOLDIER

"The object of the Sanitary Commission was to do what the government could not."

—MARY LIVERMORE,
U.S. SANITARY COMMISSION LEADER

In 1849, Elizabeth Blackwell (1821–1910) became the first woman in the United States to earn a medical degree. Early in the war, Blackwell trained nearly one hundred women of New York City's Women's Central Association of Relief to act as nurses. Under her instruction, the trainees worked for a month in the wards at the city's Bellevue Hospital. They learned about cleanliness and injury care, including how to dress wounds and how to make splints and crutches.

Within days of the Fort Sumter bombing in April 1861, a group of more than 2,000 women gathered in New York City. They called themselves the Women's Central Association of Relief for the Sick and Wounded of the Army. They were determined to ensure that their sons and husbands escaped the fate of the troops who had fought the Crimean War in Europe, five years before. In that conflict, Britain, France, and Turkey battled against Russia. For every English soldier killed in battle, at least four had died of disease.

THE SANITARY COMMISSION

An organization called the United States Sanitary Commission (USSC) grew from this initial meeting of concerned women. Its goal was to support Union troops with supplies, nurses, and medical care. To be most effective, the USSC sought to work cooperatively with the U.S. Army.

Several men who were community leaders in medicine, science, law, and the church assumed leadership of the new commission. Using personal connections and experience dealing with the U.S. government, they convinced President Lincoln and the War Department to allow the USSC to provide advice about sanitation and health to the army's medical department.

A U.S. Sanitary Commission volunteer provides comfort to a hospitalized soldier by reading to him. This illustration appeared in *Harper's Weekly*, April 9, 1864.

In July 1861, the USSC's hired physicians inspected twenty army camps around Washington. Their alarming report said "that the tents were so crowded at night that the men were poisoned by the vitiated atmosphere, that the sinks [latrines] were unnecessarily and disgustingly offensive, that personal cleanliness among the men was wholly unattended to, that the clothing was of bad material and almost always filthy." The report warned of scurvy outbreaks because the soldiers were not being fed vegetables.

The government did not immediately respond to the commission's recommendations for improving the health of the troops. But in spring 1862, Dr. William Hammond, a USSC supporter, was appointed surgeon general of the U.S. Army medical department. He implemented many positive changes, including the commission's earlier suggestions.

The USSC printed educational pamphlets written by doctors about disease prevention and injury treatment. It distributed hundreds of thousands of these to soldiers and officers. One pamphlet described the best way to set up a campsite, avoiding unhealthy drinking water, poor drainage, and overflowing latrines. Another pamphlet listed foods that prevented scurvy.

A Sanitary Commission wagon loaded with supplies prepares to leave Washington for Union camps. In letters and memoirs, soldiers, officers, and doctors expressed their gratitude to the USSC for bringing clothing, nurses, helpers, and medical supplies to the battlefield hospitals. "Too much praise cannot be bestowed on this great and good institution," said one Union surgeon after the Battle of Antietam.

The Sanitary Commission raised millions of dollars, in large part through the efforts of thousands of local aid societies organized by women. The groups ran Sanitary Fairs, at which they collected donations of money, food, clothing, blankets, homemade bandages, and other items for the soldiers. The societies gathered anti-scurvy vegetables that could be shipped to soldiers without spoiling, such as potatoes, cabbages, carrots, and beets. They publicized the food drives with signs: "Don't send your sweetheart a love letter. Send him an onion."

TO THE RESCUE

Smaller organizations with the same mission as the USSC assisted the U.S. Army, too. The Western Sanitary Commission operated in the Midwest, around the Mississippi River. Like the USSC, it was supported by many local women's aid societies.

A U.S. Christian Commission headquarters near a Union camp, in 1863. The evergreen boughs over the tents provided shade and some shelter from rain.

USSC female nurses, male officers, and other volunteers pose at their headquarters in Fredericksburg in May 1864, ready to assist after the Virginia battles that month.

The U.S. Christian Commission was started by members of the Young Men's Christian Association (YMCA) in November 1861. The group delivered food and medical supplies to the soldiers. As a religious organization, it also handed out Bibles and hymnbooks, held worship services in the camps, and cared for soldiers of all faiths.

The South did not have a central group comparable to the northern commissions. Individual county and state relief associations supported Confederate soldiers. Just as in the North, these aid societies—usually organized by women—provided bandages, blankets, clothing, food, and volunteer nurses. They raised money through concerts, fairs, and raffles.

At the beginning of the war, few people anticipated how important the aid societies and commissions would become. Soon the armies engaged in huge battles, some with 20,000 casualties—or more. The volunteer groups set up headquarters and hospitals near battlefields to assist the masses of injured men. They rushed much-needed supplies and helpers to the scene.

But often it wasn't enough. The wounds were devastating. The carnage was appalling. The medical departments of both armies were overwhelmed.

Wounded Union soldiers and a volunteer nurse gather outside a USSC center in Fredericksburg. It was established to provide support and care for men injured in Virginia's bloody Battle of the Wilderness in May 1864.

WOMEN OF THE

MARY LIVERMORE
(1820–1905)

Mary Livermore spent her early life in Boston before moving with her husband and children to Illinois about ten years before the Civil War began. With the war's outbreak, she became active in the Sanitary Commission's Chicago branch, traveling throughout the Midwest to establish women's aid societies. In October 1863, she organized a large, successful Sanitary Fair in Chicago.

As Livermore visited military camps, she wrote columns for her husband's Chicago newspaper. Readers were interested in what their sons and husbands were experiencing, and Livermore's skillful writing was popular. Her columns also included letters she received from the front lines.

The first time she entered a military hospital, in St. Louis, Livermore was shaken by the wounds. She had to rush out of the ward to compose herself. "Three times I returned," she recalled, "and each time some new horror smote my vision, some more sickening odor nauseated me." She forced herself "to remain in the ward without nausea or faintness" until she got used to the "shocking sights that are the outcome of the wicked business men call war."

Livermore became the eyes of the USSC along the Mississippi River. When she saw that troops and hospitals needed supplies, she used her letters and columns to rally the aid societies into action. She recruited nurses and rolled up her sleeves to care for soldiers herself.

After the war, Livermore put her organizational and writing skills to work in the fight for women's right to vote. She served as president of several state and national suffrage organizations, giving speeches and writing articles for newspapers. Livermore also pushed for reforms in women's education and dress.

AID SOCIETIES

FELICIA GRUNDY PORTER
(1820–1889)

Felicia Grundy Porter was born and raised in Nashville, Tennessee, the daughter of a U.S. senator. Active in volunteer groups before the war, she knew how to organize people and raise money.

When fighting broke out, Porter dedicated herself to supporting Confederate soldiers. She served as president of the Women's Relief Society in Tennessee. By collecting financial donations from southern citizens, she helped to set up hospitals for the wounded in Nashville and to provide supplies to the troops.

After the war, Porter led organizations to establish graves for Confederates killed near Nashville and to assist amputees who needed artificial limbs.

Union surgeon Francis Eveleth
(1832–1895) of Maine (top)
Confederate surgeon
Edmund Massie (1839–1872)
of Virginia (right)

CHAPTER SIX

DOCTORS
IN
BLUE
AND GRAY

> "I had been on the field for some time
> and seen the shower of grape and cannister
> pass thick around me, hearing the whiz
> of the minie ball and crash of the
> cannonball as it passed."
>
> —WILLIAM MCPHEETERS, CONFEDERATE SURGEON

Before the war began, the U.S. Army had just over a hundred military surgeons, enough for its small force of 16,000 men. When the conflict began, about a fifth of those surgeons left to join the Confederate army in their home states. Both sides desperately needed more doctors.

As a state's volunteer regiment formed, its officers chose doctors to care for the soldiers. In many regiments, the surgeon and assistant surgeon (usually a younger, less experienced doctor) were civilians appointed because of their political or personal connections, not their medical qualifications.

Besides these commissioned surgeons and assistant surgeons, the Union and Confederate militaries hired contract doctors for temporary duty, especially in hospitals. Occasionally, local physicians volunteered to help when there was a major battle near their home.

UNPREPARED

Some of the doctors didn't have a formal medical degree. Instead, the man's education was limited to a short apprenticeship with a practicing physician. Even the ones with a degree often had meager training.

Several American medical schools required extensive course study and apprenticeships. Many others did not. At those schools, a student didn't need an undergraduate education to enroll. A graduate received a diploma after sitting in on only a few months of lectures in anatomy, chemistry, and physiology. These new doctors had no hands-on experience with patients. They hadn't observed a surgery.

Except for the surgeons who had previously served in the military, the majority of doctors entered the war without ever seeing a bullet wound. They had never treated the diseases that spread through the camps. These men were more used to delivering babies than amputating legs.

Veteran army surgeons weren't always impressed with the contract physicians and local volunteers. A Union doctor at the Battle of Fair Oaks in June 1862 wrote in his journal, "The surgeons who volunteered to come out for a short time have been of but little service. They want to perform surgical operations, but a sick man stands a poor chance with them."

Soldiers, too, dreaded being under the care of unqualified doctors. A Union soldier wrote, "There is a vast difference in surgeons; some are harsh and cruel—whether it is from habit or insensibility I am not prepared to say—but I know the men would face a rebel battery with less forebodings than they do some of our worthy surgeons."

"More of our soldiers have died from unskilled but well-paid physicians," said one North Carolinian, "than from battles with the enemy."

Military officials heard complaints about poor medical care from soldiers' families, the press, and others. The medical departments tried to weed out incompetent or negligent doctors. They required the commissioned surgeons to have a medical degree and to pass an exam that tested their knowledge. They dismissed any found to be guilty of serious offenses. Reasons for dismissal included "intemperate use of whiskey and opium," neglecting the wounded, stealing whiskey from the medical supplies and selling it to soldiers, and deserting during battle.

Still, most of the physicians who served were capable, caring, and fast learners. Both Union and Confederate medical departments distributed manuals to their doctors detailing surgical techniques and the recommended treatment of diseases and wounds. Surgeons learned from experience about sickness and injuries, improving their skills.

Fannie Beers, a Confederate hospital matron, had praise for them. She wrote, "I never saw or heard of a more self-sacrificing set of men than the surgeons I met and served under during the war."

STEWARDS

The regimental surgeons had their hands full with sick and wounded soldiers. In both armies, stewards were assigned to assist them. The medical team of many Confederate regiments, for example, had a surgeon, two assistant surgeons, a steward, and other soldiers who acted as helpers.

During fighting, a steward often went to the battlefield with an assistant surgeon to provide first aid to the wounded. He carried a knapsack of medicines and supplies that the surgeon needed.

In a hospital, the steward's job was to mix medicines prescribed by the doctors, give smallpox vaccinations, and order medical supplies. He also supervised hospital staff, including the soldiers assigned as attendants and nurses. At times, stewards administered anesthetics and assisted with surgeries.

Stewards were appointed based on their qualifications and experience. Many applicants were medical students who had not yet graduated. Others had been apprenticed to physicians but hadn't taken formal medical classes.

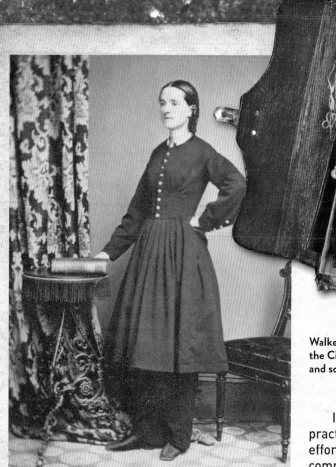

Mary Walker in a photograph from the war period, in which she wears trousers under a short skirt. She said this clothing was more practical and comfortable for the work she did. An advocate for women's dress reform, she wore men's clothes throughout her life.

DR. MARY WALKER
(1832–1919)

At the time of the Civil War, approximately 200 women in the United States had graduated from medical school. Of those who volunteered their service to the military, almost all acted as nurses because the armies wouldn't commission female surgeons. One southern woman is known to have worked as a doctor at a Confederate military hospital alongside her physician husband. Mary Walker was the sole woman to be paid by the Union army as a doctor, but she was never a commissioned military surgeon.

Walker's pocket surgical kit that she carried during the Civil War. It includes scalpels to make incisions and scissors to cut bandages.

In October 1861, Walker left her medical practice in upstate New York to help in the war effort. Because she was unable to get a surgeon commission, she volunteered in a Washington hospital. Walker nursed soldiers and assisted families who came to the city to visit their hospitalized relatives.

During the Battle of Fredericksburg, she volunteered to provide first aid on the battlefield, though she wasn't trained to perform surgery in the field hospitals. Despite criticism of her presence by some in the military, Walker gained a reputation as a skillful doctor. The army eventually hired her as an assistant surgeon, and she served in Tennessee and Kentucky. In 1864, Walker was captured and held by the Confederates for four months in a Richmond prison, where she cared for Union soldiers.

In November 1865, Walker received the Congressional Medal of Honor for her bravery. She was the first and only woman to receive it. Walker spent the rest of her life promoting women's rights, traveling and giving speeches. Her Medal of Honor was withdrawn in 1917, as were nearly a thousand others, because she had been a civilian doctor, which disqualified her for a military award. Walker refused to return her medal during her lifetime. Her honor was restored in 1977.

DR. ALEXANDER AUGUSTA
(1825–1890)

About a dozen African American physicians served with the Union army, either as commissioned military surgeons or hired contract doctors. They all were assigned to black regiments or to hospitals for black soldiers and refugees.

The first to be appointed as a commissioned army surgeon was Alexander Augusta. He was born free in Norfolk, Virginia, and later earned his medical degree in Toronto, Canada. Augusta was practicing medicine in Canada when the war broke out.

In 1863, after the U.S. Colored Troops were organized, the thirty-eight-year-old doctor requested and was granted an appointment as a surgeon for a Maryland black regiment. Later, when white physicians with less seniority complained about taking orders from him, the War Department put Augusta in charge of physical exams of black recruits.

After the war ended, Augusta practiced medicine in Washington and taught at Howard University's medical school. He is buried in Arlington National Cemetery.

A few had trained at pharmacies or studied at one of a handful of pharmacy schools. In some cases, surgeons or other stewards provided on-the-job training to a soldier interested in medical care.

DANGEROUS DUTY

Although the war offered opportunities to those looking for medical experience and a way to make a living, the work was difficult. James Benton, a twenty-five-year-old practicing New York physician, signed up as an assistant surgeon. He wrote his father in October 1862, "It is not patriotism that has made me take this course but I wanted to make money for my family. If it had been patriotism, I should have been sick of it long since."

Surgeons frequently had to operate on dozens of mangled men in one day. While visiting his wounded troops at a Gettysburg field hospital, a Union general observed the impact of war on the doctors. "A surgeon," he noted, "having been long at work, would put down his knife, exclaiming that his hand had grown unsteady, and that this was too much for human endurance—not seldom hysterical tears streaming down his face."

Medical duty was dangerous, too. Doctors and stewards were struck by bullets and exploding artillery shells while tending patients near the battlefield. By one count, more than a hundred Union surgeons died or were wounded in battle. Nearly 300 died of disease.

When an army retreated, it often was forced to leave surgeons and wounded soldiers in the enemy's hands. The captured doctors were usually allowed to continue caring for their wounded. Eventually, they were released to their regiments or were exchanged for a doctor from the other side. There were exceptions, and some doctors became prisoners of war for long periods.

By the end of the war, more than 12,000 doctors had served on the Union side, including commissioned and contract surgeons. Historians estimate that the Confederates had at least 10,000, though the records are incomplete.

Besides the illnesses that constantly plagued four million soldiers and sailors, the overworked medical teams handled hundreds of thousands of injuries.

Most were caused by one small piece of lead.

STEWARDS

Thomas H. S. Pennington (right) enlisted in a U.S. Colored Troops Infantry regiment in New York in 1864 and served as its steward. This photograph was taken in New Orleans, Louisiana, where his regiment was stationed. With surgeons in short supply during the second half of the war, black regiments usually weren't assigned as many doctors as white regiments. To make up for reduced staffing, some used a steward in a doctor's role. The army officially forbade these men from acting as surgeons because they had no medical training, either in school or an apprenticeship. But out of necessity, many took on the responsibility anyway.

A steward mixes drugs at a Union camp in this illustration from *Frank Leslie's Illustrated Newspaper*, November 12, 1864.

These stewards pose for a photographer outside tents at a Union hospital in Petersburg, Virginia, October 1864.

SURGEONS

SURGEON GENERAL WILLIAM HAMMOND
(1828–1900)

Hammond became the U.S. Army's surgeon general in April 1862, at age thirty-three. Before the war, he had been an army surgeon and medical researcher. Hammond's goal was to modernize the medical corps. He pushed for examinations to ensure that only qualified surgeons served; for a formal ambulance corps; for construction of more healthful hospitals; and for a system that encouraged surgeons to share information about injuries and disease.

One of Hammond's military orders cost him his job. He told the army's surgeons to stop using calomel, because he believed mercury harmed the body. Today, we know that he was correct. But his decision was unpopular with the doctors who relied on the medicine. With political pressure against him, Hammond was forced from his position in 1864.

GENERAL

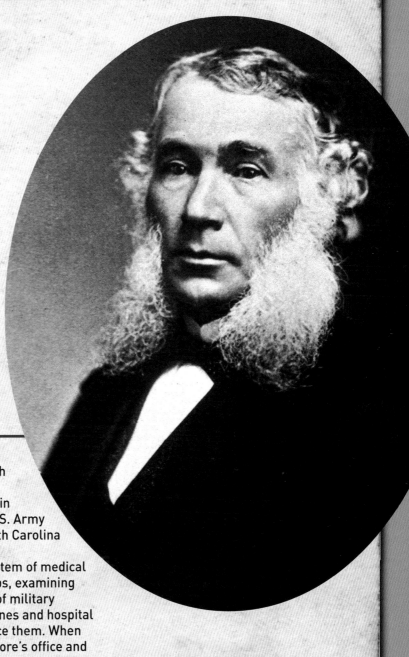

SURGEON GENERAL SAMUEL PRESTON MOORE
(1813–1889)

Born and educated in Charleston, South Carolina, Moore was appointed the Confederate army's surgeon general in July 1861. Before the war, he had been a U.S. Army doctor. He resigned that position when South Carolina seceded.

As surgeon general, Moore set up a system of medical and hospital inspectors, an ambulance corps, examining boards for surgeons, and the construction of military hospitals. To cope with shortages of medicines and hospital supplies, he established factories to produce them. When Richmond burned at the end of the war, Moore's office and its records were destroyed.

Lifeless soldiers lie where they fell at Gettysburg, July 1–3, 1863. More than 50,000 men were wounded, killed, or captured during the battle. After clashes, the victorious army usually allowed the other side to bury its dead. But sometimes days passed before bodies were retrieved or buried. Soldiers had already stripped the corpses of much-needed clothes and boots and other valuables, and the bodies had begun to decompose.

CHAPTER SEVEN

THE MURDEROUS MINIÉ

> "I felt a sharp sting in my face . . .
> Blood began to flow down my face and neck
> and I knew that I had been wounded."
>
> —RICE BULL, UNION SOLDIER

Wilbur Fisk was almost twenty-two when he enlisted in the Union army. His Vermont regiment fought in many of the war's bloodiest battles, and he saw his friends wounded and killed. In May 1864, as the Union army moved toward Richmond, Fisk witnessed the slaughter at the Battle of the Wilderness. Soldiers shot at close range, mowing each other down.

"The rebels were one side of the breastwork, and we on the other," he wrote to his hometown newspaper. "We could touch their guns with ours. They would load, jump up and fire into us, and we did the same to them. Almost every shot that was made took effect. . . . Our men lay piled one top of another, nearly all shot through the head."

CARNAGE

As the war continued month after bloody month, Americans—northern and southern, civilian and military—were stunned by the number of casualties. In some estimates, more than 200,000 Union and Confederate soldiers died from battlefield injuries.

Communities everywhere received the devastating news of hometown boys falling in battle. Public anxiety was heightened by horrifying photographs of the carnage, taken by Mathew Brady, Alexander Gardner, James Gibson, Timothy O'Sullivan, George Barnard, and others.

Soldiers attacking in close formation were easy targets for the enemy. In one tragic example, at Gettysburg, more than 12,000 Confederates advanced across nearly a mile of open field toward Union positions on a hill. An hour later, after a storm of lead from Union guns, about half of the Rebels had been wounded, killed, or captured. The disastrous assault later became known as Pickett's Charge, after General George Pickett, whose division was one of three ordered by General Robert E. Lee to make the attack.

The Minié ball, the bullet that wounded and killed tens of thousands of men in the Civil War

FLYING METAL

During the war, bayonets and sabers killed fewer than a thousand Union soldiers in battle. Guns were far deadlier.

A cannon's exploding shell peppered soldiers with metal that sliced through their bodies. Most victims died instantly.

A Confederate soldier described his experience with artillery at the Battle of Antietam: "A shell burst not ten feet above the Seventeenth, where the men were lying prone on their faces; it literally tore to pieces poor Appich . . . mangling his body terribly and spattering his blood over many who were lying around him."

Cannons were lethal, but of all the battlefield wounds that surgeons treated, most were from rifles shooting one particular kind of bullet—the Minié ball. This bullet had been developed a dozen years earlier, in 1849, by Frenchman Claude-Étienne Minié. It was easier to load into a gun and could be shot farther and with more accuracy than other bullets. It also caused more serious injuries.

Because the Minié ball was made of soft lead, it flattened when it hit the body, shattering bones and ripping flesh, muscle, and blood vessels. Besides the physical damage, the bullet often picked up foreign material as it entered the body, such as sweat and clothing fibers. That led to infections.

STOP THE BLOOD!

Before a battle began, the armies prepared for the inevitable casualties. A regiment's assistant surgeon, steward, and a few soldiers assigned to the medical team set up a first aid, or field dressing, station close to the firing line. They chose a protected spot in a building, behind a small hill, or among the trees. The steward brought a knapsack full of supplies: bandages, sponges, a scalpel, thread, tourniquets, opium pills and morphine, and whiskey or brandy.

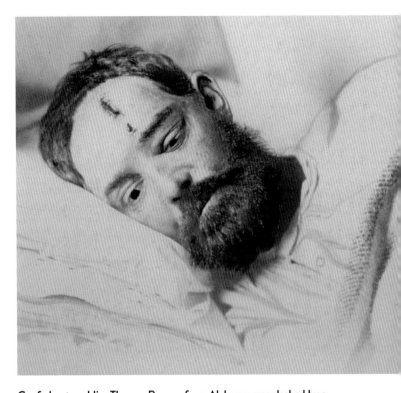

Confederate soldier Thomas Rogers, from Alabama, was slashed by a saber on April 2, 1865, near Petersburg. The forty-one-year-old man was captured, and a Union surgeon in Washington removed fractured skull bone pressing on his brain. Rogers remained in a Union hospital until he recovered.

Once the shooting started, the battlefield became a loud, chaotic scene with thundering guns, galloping horses, and screaming men. When a soldier was hurt, he made his way to the field dressing station.

If he was unable to walk on his own, a fellow soldier often assisted him. Army officials noticed that these helpful men couldn't be trusted to return to battle. To keep them in the fight, officers either hired ambulance drivers or assigned regimental musicians (such as drummers and buglers) to fetch the injured. The rescuers carried disabled men on stretchers. When they ran out of stretchers, they improvised with blankets, doors, ladders, gates, and other items they found nearby.

Unfortunately, the rescuers frequently panicked and ran away. They had good reason to be frightened. As stretcher bearers ventured onto the battlefield in the midst of the action, they were sometimes hit by bullets and artillery shells.

At the dressing station, the medical team wrapped minor wounds with cloth bandages and gave the injured water to drink. Soldiers were parched because of blood loss and strenuous combat. After a man with a slight wound was patched up, he was sent back into battle.

For more serious injuries, such as gunshot wounds, the surgeon tried to stop the bleeding by using a tourniquet or applying pressure. If that didn't work, he tied thread around the gushing blood vessel. He picked out anything that had been driven into the bullet hole, such as grass, dirt, or cloth from the uniform. The medical team protected the injury by packing it with lint (fibers scraped from linen cloth). Then they bandaged it. If an arm or leg bone had been broken, the medical team immobilized it with a wood splint.

The soldier might be given a drink of whiskey or brandy to calm him and prevent shock. For pain relief, he received opium pills or morphine, which often was sprinkled into open wounds .

None of this was done in a sanitary way. Doctors realized that foreign material in a wound would complicate healing, but they didn't know that microbes caused infection. Everyone's hands were filthy.

The medical team usually could tell when an injury was mortal. With suffering soldiers lined up, they had to focus on the ones who could be saved. Men who had been hit in the chest or abdomen rarely survived. In the 1860s, surgeons didn't cut into the chest or abdominal cavity to remove a bullet or make repairs. Experience had taught them that if the surgery didn't kill the patient, infection would. Bullets striking the head and spine would probably kill the victim, too. Doctors weren't able to treat severe damage there, either.

A Confederate steward at the First Battle of Bull Run later wrote about a soldier hit in the mouth by a metal fragment from an exploding shell: "We commenced dressing the wound but before we had done anything others were brought out and being desperately hurt we left him to attend them."

A dying man was given morphine or whiskey to keep him comfortable. Then he was laid to the side.

Soldiers with serious but treatable injuries were sent to a field hospital safely outside of artillery range. They would receive more extensive care and surgery there. Wagons pulled by horses carried the wounded away from the fighting. The trip over rutted, bumpy roads felt like torture. Sometimes a wagon became unbalanced and dumped its patients. Soldiers called these ambulances gutbusters.

This illustration by artist Winslow Homer appeared in *Harper's Weekly*, July 1862. It shows a medical team tending to the wounded at a field dressing station. Smoke from the battle rises in the background. The steward stands in the middle carrying a knapsack on his back from which a doctor is removing supplies. In the left and right backgrounds, men carry the wounded on stretchers. An ambulance wagon waits.

LEFT TO DIE

The Battle of Fair Oaks was fought May 31 and June 1, 1862, on the Virginia Peninsula. More than 10,000 men were killed or wounded. Many stretcher bearers and ambulance drivers headed to the rear for safety, failing to rescue the injured.

Union soldiers lay in swampy marshes for three or four days, some dying before anyone helped them. Search parties later found survivors who had crawled to drier ground but didn't have the strength to go farther.

The Confederate army left wounded behind, too. After the gunfire stopped, women from Richmond, a few miles away, took carriages to the battlefield and camps to gather the fallen who were still alive. They brought them to hospitals and private homes for nursing.

Fair Oaks was one of several battles fought on the Virginia Peninsula during the spring and summer of 1862. The North's attempt to invade Richmond was a military failure, and the army was forced to retreat. The Peninsula Campaign was a fiasco for the Union's medical department, too. In addition to those injured in action, thousands of soldiers had fallen ill with malaria, diarrhea, typhoid fever, and scurvy during three months in the rain and muck.

As wounded and sick Union soldiers waited to be evacuated from the Peninsula, they filled poorly supplied, improvised field hospitals along the James River. One observer described the scene: "They lay in thousands around the premises, upon the wet ground . . . All day and all night they remained in this exposed situation, many of them hurried out of the world

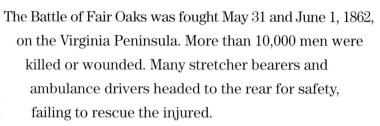

Samuel Wright from Massachusetts joined the Union army in May 1861 when he was eighteen. For three years, he fought in brutal battles and was wounded at least four times. During the Battle of Antietam, Wright tore down a wooden fence that blocked a Union charge—while Confederates shot at him. For his bravery, he was awarded the Medal of Honor.

At the Battle of Petersburg in June 1864, a Minié ball struck Wright's right eye and broke the surrounding bone. Shots to the head were usually fatal, and he was left for dead. But Wright survived again.

A surgeon managed to remove the bullet. After eight months, Wright had healed enough to be discharged from the hospital and finish his recovery at home. His eye had been destroyed, and he wore a patch over it until his death at age sixty-three.

by this neglect. . . . Everybody declares that the Medical Department, as now organized, is a disgraceful failure."

The U.S. Sanitary Commission saved the day. It arranged for a small fleet of boats—fitted with food, medical necessities, doctors, and nurses— to transport these men to northern hospitals.

The debacle showed military leaders that their medical system was dangerously flawed. Battlefield rescue and hospital care had been disastrous. Help for the sick and wounded was haphazard and often ineffective.

Something had to be done—and fast.

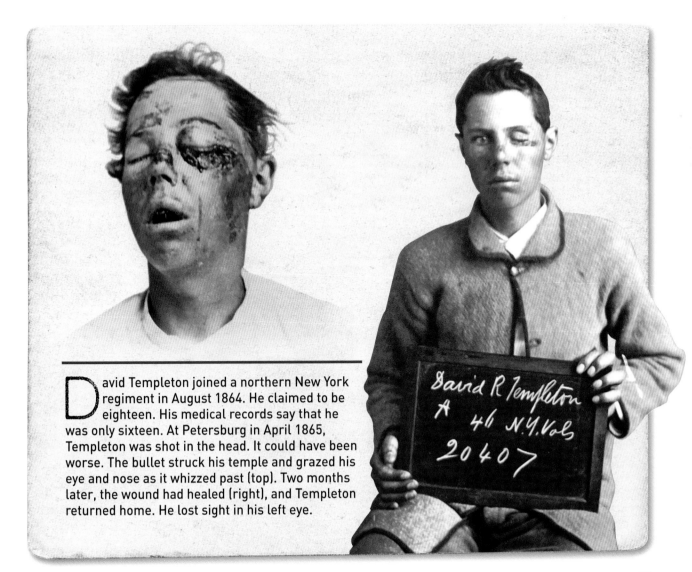

David Templeton joined a northern New York regiment in August 1864. He claimed to be eighteen. His medical records say that he was only sixteen. At Petersburg in April 1865, Templeton was shot in the head. It could have been worse. The bullet struck his temple and grazed his eye and nose as it whizzed past (top). Two months later, the wound had healed (right), and Templeton returned home. He lost sight in his left eye.

An illustration of the Battle of Antietam, September 17, 1862, published twenty-six years later. More Americans were killed, wounded, or listed as missing on that single day than in any other one-day battle of the war—about 23,000.

RESCUING
THE
WOUNDED

"It would seem to be perfectly suicidal
in the Government . . . not to have a corps enlisted
or detailed, to save as many as can be saved."

—HENRY BOWDITCH, PHYSICIAN AND PROFESSOR

Union army surgeon John Brinton, twenty-nine, saw his first battle just two months after being stationed along the Mississippi River. On November 7, 1861, he accompanied about 3,000 soldiers in an attack on a Confederate camp during the Battle of Belmont, Missouri.

Almost 400 Union soldiers were injured and about 100 killed. Brinton had only a few wagons to transport wounded soldiers to safety. Many who had been shot in the legs or body couldn't walk. Doctors used their own horses to carry some of the wounded away. The rest were captured.

"Had the medical officers been well supplied with ambulance wagons," Brinton complained in an official report, they would not have had to abandon the men—"a most mortifying circumstance."

An illustration of the Union retreat after its defeat in the Second Battle of Bull Run, August 1862. Thousands of Union wounded were left behind on the battlefield, unable to move. Ambulances sent to rescue the men broke down, or their drivers ran away. Some of the injured lay in the open with no food for five days during cold, rainy weather. Many died before help arrived.

CLEARING THE BATTLEFIELD

Doctors knew that soldiers died when they didn't get medical attention fast enough. But the army medical departments were frustrated in their efforts to improve battlefield rescues.

An army's quartermaster department, responsible for providing supplies, was in charge of assigning ambulances. Yet the quartermaster usually gave priority to weapons and ammunition, not to medical needs. The early battles of the war exposed the suffering that occurred when the quartermaster denied surgeons' requests for ambulances.

Dr. Jonathan Letterman proposed a solution. He was able to put his plan into action after Surgeon General Hammond appointed him medical director of the Union's Army of the Potomac, led by General George McClellan. McClellan had seen the damaging effect of poor medical care on an army while visiting Europe during the Crimean War. He wholeheartedly supported Letterman's new system.

The plan gave control of ambulances to the medical department. Each division within the Army of the Potomac had its own ambulance corps. A division varied in size from 7,000 to 10,000 soldiers and included nine or more regiments. Each regiment was allotted at least three ambulances.

When a battle was anticipated, the medical director gave instructions for placing ambulances at locations where they could best rescue the wounded. Each ambulance was manned by two soldiers and a driver. Letterman wanted responsible, brave men in this role. To be chosen for the ambulance crew, a soldier had "to be active and efficient."

Under the Letterman system, ambulance teams drilled regularly. Here, a Union ambulance crew trains as fellow soldiers pretend to be injured. Some of the men wear the Zouave uniform.

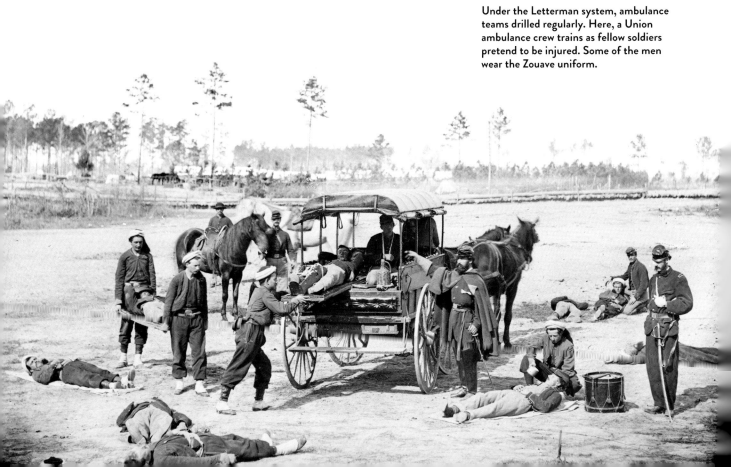

An artist created this etching, "In the hands of the enemy after Gettysburg," many years after the battle. A Union surgeon attends to the leg wound of a Confederate soldier in a Gettysburg home while the family offers solace. Local residents often helped care for the wounded from both sides. They supplied water, food, and bandages made from strips of their tablecloths and sheets. Locals also assisted with burials.

Only designated stretcher bearers were supposed to remove the wounded from the battlefield. An uninjured soldier was permitted to carry a comrade just a few yards back from the action. Then he had to return immediately to the fight.

Ambulance crews were specially trained. They learned the best way to lift men from the ground, carry them on stretchers, and move them into and out of ambulances. After a seriously injured soldier received first aid at a dressing station, an ambulance crew transferred him to the field hospital.

Letterman's system had its first major test in September 1862 at the Battle of Antietam. Ambulance crews rescued the Union wounded from the battlefield and transported them to field hospitals within twenty-four hours of the fighting's end. Considering the battle's unprecedented casualties that day, this was a huge improvement over the Second Battle of Bull Run a few weeks earlier.

By Gettysburg, a three-day battle on July 1, 2, and 3, 1863, the system was even more efficient. Letterman reported that nearly all the Union wounded were removed from the field by the morning of July 4.

AMBULANCES FOR ALL

Letterman's ambulance system officially applied only to part of the Union army—the Army of the Potomac. Surgeon General Hammond proposed expanding the ambulance corps to the entire Union army. But the top commanding general vetoed the plan. He thought that the cost of more ambulances outweighed the advantages. The U.S. Sanitary Commission also lobbied for an army-wide ambulance corps, without success.

Another advocate was Henry Bowditch (1808–1892) of Boston, an influential physician, abolitionist, and Harvard University professor. While spending a short time as a volunteer surgeon near Washington in 1862, Bowditch was appalled at the incompetence of the ambulance drivers.

But it was personal tragedy that propelled him to fight tenaciously for a Union army ambulance corps. In March 1863, his twenty-three-year-old son Nathaniel was shot in the abdomen multiple times during a Virginia battle. Although young Bowditch lay a safe distance from enemy lines where he could have been easily rescued, no stretcher bearers arrived. The next day, he died from his wounds. His grieving father believed that Nathaniel would have lived had an ambulance corps of capable men been there in time to take him to medical care.

Ambulances prepare to transport the wounded after a Virginia battle. Letterman's system called for ambulance crews to be in place near the battlefield, ready for rescues. Each division was responsible for maintaining its own ambulances.

Henry Bowditch pushed the president, the secretary of war, and Congress to establish an army-wide ambulance corps like the one Letterman proposed. When that effort failed, Bowditch rallied support from newspapers and medical journals. He published a pamphlet in which he wrote that the government must establish "a corps of honest, brave, and humane men, enlisted for this special duty."

Letterman replaced many of the two-wheeled gutbuster ambulances used at the start of the war with four-wheeled wagons that carried more soldiers more comfortably. The Union tried several styles designed to be lighter and easier for horses to pull. Springs made the ride on bumpy roads less jarring to the wounded. This model carried both sitting and lying soldiers.

Bowditch's campaign, combined with public pressure from the Sanitary Commission and others, finally led Congress to override the objections of the war department and top generals. It passed a law establishing the U.S. Army ambulance corps under control of the medical department. The law took effect on March 11, 1864.

WHO GOES FIRST?

Another part of Letterman's rescue plan was to identify the wounded who most needed care and to make sure they were treated quickly. A similar approach had been used during recent European wars. Some army surgeons already followed the procedure, but it was not official.

Under Letterman's system, surgeons divided the wounded into three groups:

1. Those whose injuries were not life-threatening. They could wait for attention.

2. Those who had serious wounds that could be treated. Help them first.

3. Those whose wounds were so devastating that the soldier would certainly die. Set these men aside and keep them comfortable.

This evaluation of injuries occurred at the battlefield dressing station and again at the field hospital. It saved lives, but the approach wasn't foolproof. During the chaos of a battle, when surgeons and their assistants were overloaded with injuries to treat, they were forced to make snap decisions. They made mistakes. At times, men who seemed mortally wounded and were placed to the side could have been saved.

The Confederate army followed a system similar to Letterman's for prioritizing treatment of injuries and evacuating the wounded. The Confederates never had enough ambulance wagons, however, and they often had to use farm wagons instead. The wounded suffered as their bodies were shaken up on rough rural roads. Whenever possible, the Rebels captured better-equipped Union ambulances.

Tents at a Union field hospital on a farm field, after the Battle of Antietam. Union doctors are caring for captured Confederate wounded, who lie on straw inside the tents. A nearby barn was part of this field hospital.

LEFT FOR DEAD

J udson Spofford was only sixteen when he joined a Vermont regiment in July 1862. Late one afternoon, during a March 1865 battle at Petersburg, he was shot in the chest.

When Spofford was brought to the field hospital, a surgeon proclaimed him mortally wounded. Gunshots to the chest were usually fatal because of damage to the heart and lungs. Bleeding, Spofford was left outside on the ground, while other soldiers were carried in for surgery.

Spofford wasn't about to give up. He had turned nineteen just two weeks before, and he wasn't through with his life yet. Later that cold night, he begged a soldier who walked by to take him inside so that he didn't freeze to death. Once Spofford was in the hospital, an assistant cleaned away the blood and a surgeon took another look at the wound.

Miraculously, the Minié ball had entered the right side of Spofford's chest, sliced through the skin layers on its way out the other side, and lodged in his arm. With a simple scalpel cut, the surgeon lifted out the bullet. Spofford asked to keep it as a memento. He went on to a long, successful life as a businessman and was buried in Arlington National Cemetery when he died at ninety-one.

As medical director of the Union's Army of the Potomac, Jonathan Letterman was in charge of the health of about 100,000 soldiers.

JONATHAN LETTERMAN
(1824–1872)

Born in Pennsylvania, Jonathan Letterman followed in his father's footsteps and studied medicine. After graduating from medical school in Philadelphia, Letterman joined the army as a doctor in June 1849 at age twenty-four. He spent thirteen years as an army surgeon at western outposts.

In January 1862, the U.S. Army assigned Letterman as a medical director of Union troops in western Virginia. During this time, he became better acquainted with William Hammond, who was impressed by Letterman's medical views and organizational skills.

Soon after Hammond took over as U.S. Army surgeon general in April 1862, he faced the medical disaster on the Virginia Peninsula. The new surgeon general turned to Letterman, appointing him medical director of the Army of the Potomac that summer.

After eighteen months of hard work improving the care of soldiers, Letterman's responsibilities took a toll on his health. In December 1863, he asked to be transferred from his position. He didn't state his reasons, but some believed it was partly because Surgeon General Hammond—Letterman's friend and chief supporter—was being forced out. Letterman served as an army hospital inspector in Pennsylvania for a while, eventually resigning from the army in December 1864.

Letterman moved to California with his wife, where he practiced medicine, acted as San Francisco's coroner, and unsuccessfully invested in oil drilling. In October 1867, his wife died suddenly, leaving him with two little girls, ages one and three. Letterman had suffered from chronic dysentery since the war, and his health was fragile. In March 1872, less than five years after his wife's death, he died at age forty-seven.

Today, Letterman's system is used by the military and by civilian emergency responders. Known as *triage*, this approach efficiently sorts the injured so that the most seriously wounded, who are likely to die without immediate treatment, are cared for first. Because of his contributions during the Civil War, Letterman has been called the Father of Battlefield Medicine.

Opposite: Letterman (seated, left) with his staff.

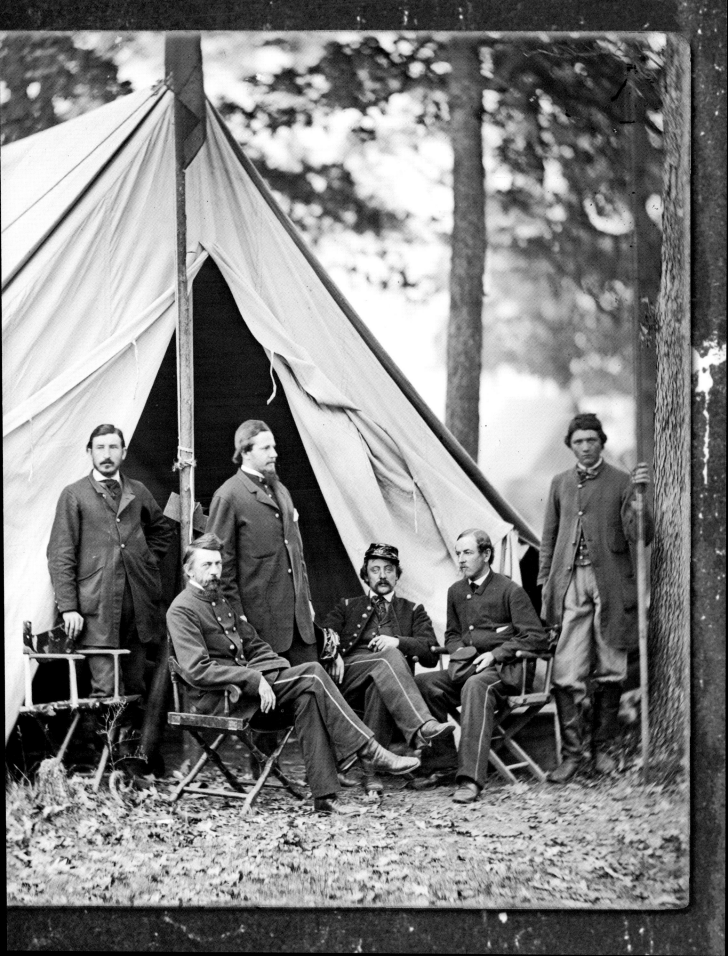

A Union field hospital at City Point, Virginia. Hospitals were often located next to railroad lines so that trains could move supplies in and move the wounded out to general hospitals. Stays at field hospitals were meant to be temporary.

ON TO THE FIELD HOSPITAL

Ambulances or stretcher bearers transported the seriously wounded from the dressing stations to a field hospital. This was where doctors performed surgery.

Although the number of staff members varied, each field hospital usually had a chief surgeon, three or four surgeons who operated on the wounded, and nine or more assistant surgeons. The operating surgeons, often including the chief surgeon, were the doctors with the most skill. Some assistant surgeons helped with operations and administered the anesthetic. Others dressed wounds and kept records of surgeries, treatments, and deaths. The hospital's staff also included stewards and soldiers assigned to be nurses.

Before a battle began, the chief surgeon picked a place for the field hospital. It had to be close to the fighting but safely out of the enemy's artillery range, at least a mile away. He wanted a structure large enough to handle many wounded and well ventilated, to prevent deadly miasma from accumulating.

Field hospitals were set up in houses, schools, and churches. Doctors also used barns, sheds, and tents, which had good ventilation. At the Battle of Antietam, Union surgeons established more than seventy field hospitals to handle all the wounded. The Confederate medical department took over the nearby town of Shepherdstown in what is now West Virginia. One resident remembered that soldiers "filled every building and overflowed into the country round, into farm-houses, barns, corn-cribs, cabins,—wherever four walls and a roof were found together."

Sometimes a field hospital wasn't far enough away from the fighting.

Savage's Station, a field hospital next to the railroad on the Virginia Peninsula. This photograph, taken on June 27, 1862, shows about twenty Union surgeons and assistants tending the wounded and sick. As the rest of the Union army retreated and Confederate forces approached, these doctors stayed behind with 2,500 men who were too weak to move. They all became prisoners of war.

During the Battle of Chancellorsville, a Union surgeon was forced to move back several times as Confederate troops closed in on him. "The shell fell pretty thick around me at first but that soon stopped and I went to operating. When we fell back I narrowly escaped being captured." Artillery fire killed one of his assistants.

In big battles with many casualties, even Letterman's trained ambulance corps couldn't keep up. The sheer numbers of maimed soldiers overwhelmed the ambulance crews and medical staffs on both sides. Men were left on the battleground.

In June 1864, nearly two years after Letterman introduced the ambulance corps, the wounded at the Battle of Cold Harbor lay on the battlefield for several days. A Union nurse was shocked when she saw the men finally brought to the field hospital "with blood oozing from their torn flesh, and worms literally covering the festering wounds—dying with thirst, starving for food . . . groaning in delirious fever, praying to die, to be rid of the intense pain which racked the poor body."

It was up to the surgeons, working at field hospital operating tables, to save the lives of these battered soldiers.

An illustration depicting a Union field hospital, likely during an 1862 battle. At the center, an ambulance wagon delivers wounded to the house. The medical team performs operations on a table outside. Wounded men lie against the building, either waiting their turn or waiting to die. A red or yellow flag was placed on the roof to show the enemy that it was a field hospital and not to be fired on. The artist, Thomas Nast, described the scene: "The air resounds with shrieks of agony, and the ground near the surgeon's table is strewed with amputated limbs."

CHAPTER NINE

UNDER
THE
KNIFE

> "Every house, for miles around, is a hospital and
> I have seen arms, legs, feet and hands lying in piles
> rotting in the blazing heat ... and still the knife went
> steadily in its work adding to the putrid mess."
>
> —DANIEL M. HOLT, UNION ASSISTANT SURGEON, AFTER THE BATTLE OF ANTIETAM

As the battle raged nearby, Union general Carl Schurz checked on his men at the division's field hospital. He was overcome with emotion by what he saw and heard. "The stretchers coming in dreadful procession from the bloody field," he recalled, "their blood-stained burdens to be unloaded at the places where the surgeons stand with their medicine chests and bandages, and their knives and uprolled sleeves and blood-smeared aprons, and by their sides ghastly heaps of cut-off legs and arms—and oh! the shrieks and wailings of the wounded men."

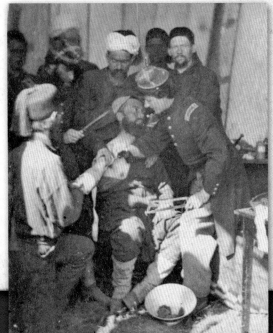

A medical team demonstrates an arm amputation in 1861. Surgeons often operated in front of many witnesses, unnerving the wounded waiting their turn. One journalist described the constant "grating of the murderous saw."

GRIM AND GRISLY

No matter where they were located—tents, houses, barns, churches—Civil War field hospitals were full of blood and death. Most of the war's surgeries were performed there.

A journalist visited a Union field hospital during the June 1862 Battle of Gaines's Mill, Virginia. "The wounded lay in the yard and lane, under the shade," he wrote, "waiting their turns to be hacked and maimed."

A young girl never forgot her experience in a house used as a field hospital after the Battle of Antietam. Along with other townspeople, she had volunteered to care for wounded Confederate soldiers. Sickened by what she saw and smelled in the upstairs rooms, she had to hang over the staircase, trying to catch her breath and regain her composure.

The wooden operating table was set up outside where the light was better. After a battle, surgeons had to work fast to save all the soldiers whose bodies had been shredded by Minié bullets. In this posed photograph, an assistant holds a cloth over the patient's face to show how anesthesia was administered. A U.S. Army medical wagon is in the background.

J. Franklin Dyer was the Union surgeon in charge of the Lacy House, a mansion taken over as a Union field hospital during the Battle of Fredericksburg, in December 1862. Hundreds of bleeding men were brought to the hospital from the battlefield. The medical crew covered the floor with straw to soak up the blood and to provide a soft surface where the wounded could lie.

There wasn't enough room for them all. Despite the cold weather, many of the injured were put outside in tents. To keep them as warm as possible, the hospital's soldier-attendants handed out blankets and spread pine boughs on the ground under the tents for insulation.

The surgeons chose one room of the house for operations. "For six days," Dyer wrote his wife, "the tables have been occupied from morning until late at night."

Doctors struggled to treat all the soldiers streaming into a field hospital. Surgeons were forced to attend first to the most serious wounds, operating on men to save lives. Soldiers with open wounds sometimes didn't get attention for days, and their wounds became infected.

A surgeon from South Carolina described the scene at a Confederate hospital during the Second Battle of Bull Run. "I saw large numbers of wounded lying on the ground . . . They were groaning and crying out with pain . . . We continued to operate until late at night and attended to all our wounded. I was very tired and slept on the ground."

A few days after the Battle of Gettysburg, a Union surgeon wrote his wife, "I am covered with blood and am tired out almost completely . . . I have been operating all day long and have got the chief part of the butchering done in a satisfactory manner."

ON THE OPERATING TABLE

Both armies followed the same procedure when an injured soldier arrived at the field hospital. Nurses and assistants sponged the wounds with water to wash away blood and mud. The sponge had already been used on dozens of other patients that day.

Attendants lifted the wounded man, who was probably screaming in pain, onto a table where the surgeon could work on him. For the best light, the table was placed next to a window or taken outside.

As the surgeon examined the wound, he quickly determined how serious it was. Had the damage been caused by an artillery shell? Was it a gunshot injury, and was a bullet still inside? Was a bone broken?

Doctors didn't have X-rays to see inside the body. The surgeon searched by sticking his unwashed finger or a metal probe into the bullet hole. He checked for any debris stuck in the wound—a fragment of clothing driven in by a bullet; a splinter of wood, metal, or bone; mud or plant material. If he could, he took it out with his fingers or forceps.

Should he operate? When the bullet had passed through the body and no bones were broken, the wound could be cleaned out and bandaged. Otherwise, surgery might be needed to remove the bullet, to stop the bleeding, or to sew up the wound.

Of gunshot victims who made it to surgery, two of three had been hit in the leg or arm. (A bullet wound in the torso or head was more likely to be fatal.)

Consulting surgeons gather around a patient as the operating surgeon prepares to cut. This scene, at Gettysburg, was probably staged for the camera. One observer described an amputation: "The surgeon snatched his knife from between his teeth . . . wiped it rapidly once or twice across his blood-stained apron, and the cutting began. The operation accomplished, the surgeon would look around with a deep sigh, and then—'Next!'"

Surgeons knew that when a bullet had broken a bone so that bone pierced the skin, they couldn't fix the damage. If the injury was not expected to heal, the limb would have to be cut off.

In the years before the war, surgery was rare. At Massachusetts General in Boston, one of the country's most prestigious hospitals, the surgeons performed fewer than 200 operations a year. Yet during a Civil War battle, surgeons at a field hospital did more than that in several hours. According to official estimates made shortly after the war, Union doctors alone performed at least 80,000 surgeries.

Many operations were amputations. According to Union records, Yankee surgeons performed about 30,000 amputations. Historians estimate that Confederate numbers were similar. Most were done in the field hospitals soon after the injury. Within a day was best. Surgeons learned from experience that the longer they waited, the higher the chances that the patient would die from extensive bleeding or infection. The wounded who were operated on two days or more after their injury had the lowest survival rates.

A round musket ball embedded in the bone of a soldier's leg, which was later amputated. Bones shattered by bullets didn't heal. Instead, they became infected, usually killing the patient. Amputation was the best option to save the soldier's life.

An alternative to amputation was called excision, or resection. The surgeon removed the damaged part of the bone instead of cutting off the entire arm or leg. The limb was splinted in the hope that the bone ends would grow into each other. But that usually didn't happen.

For several reasons, Civil War doctors performed fewer excisions than amputations. Excision surgery and recovery took longer. Field hospital surgeons frantically coping with a flood of wounded didn't have time for the procedure. The risks of death from the surgery and subsequent infection were also greater than with amputation. Many survivors of excision couldn't use the limb again anyway.

KNOCKED OUT

Most Civil War surgeries—95 percent—were completed while the patient was under anesthesia. Surgeons administered either chloroform or ether, or a combination. The two drugs had been used in operations since the late 1840s.

Chloroform was the choice in three-quarters of the cases. It worked faster and required a lower dose to put a man to sleep. Ether was more flammable. With the explosives and gunpowder on the battlefield and with lighting by candles and gas lamps, ether could be dangerous.

Methods for administering the anesthetic varied. A common way was to fold a cloth into a cone shape and place the wide end over the patient's mouth and nose. The surgeon's assistant then dripped liquid chloroform or ether onto the cloth. Just a few drops made a man unconscious and unable to feel pain. Metal funnels and other devices held over the nose and mouth reduced the evaporation of the anesthetic into the air. These were sometimes used to conserve the drugs, especially by the Confederates.

The anesthetic often caused patients to moan and flail about. When this happened, assistants held them down so that the surgeon could work. Witnesses to the operations assumed that the men were conscious and feeling pain, but they were not.

Surgeons knew that giving too much anesthetic could be lethal. They worked fast before it wore off. During the war, very few died men from being overanesthetized.

A patient is anesthetized using a metal funnel held over his nose and mouth. The surgeon's assistant dripped chloroform or ether onto a sponge or cloth at the top of the funnel. Confederate surgeon J. Julian Chisolm developed this two-inch-long device (right) to conserve precious chloroform. The drug was dripped onto cloth located behind the small round screen, and the patient breathed it in through the nose tubes.

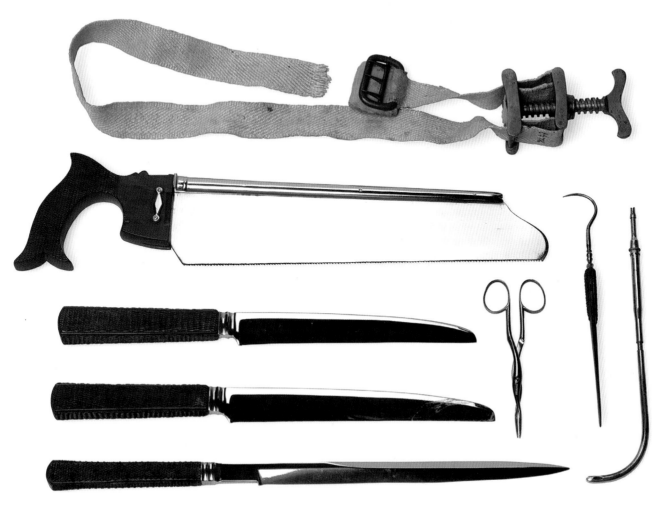

Many of these surgeon's tools from the Civil War, including the bone saw and knives, are similar to what surgeons use today when performing amputations. A tourniquet, at the top, stopped the bleeding while the surgeon cut off the limb.

A CUT ABOVE

Historians estimate that Civil War surgeons performed approximately 60,000 amputations. About a quarter of the patients died. A soldier's chance of surviving improved the farther the cut was made from his torso. Two-thirds of the men whose lower legs were amputated lived. Less than one in five survived an amputation near the hip.

An experienced surgeon could amputate a limb in less than ten minutes. First, a tourniquet was applied above the area to be cut. This stopped the bleeding until the surgeon finished. Next, he used an amputation knife to cut

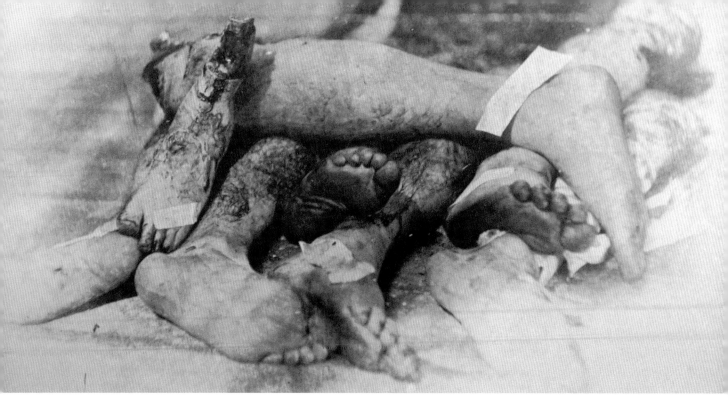

Dr. Reed B. Bontecou photographed patients at Washington's Harewood General Hospital in order to document cases for medical research and teaching. He took this photograph in 1865, labelling it "Floor of operating room after a morning's work."

Poet and author Walt Whitman, volunteering at a field hospital, described the scene after surgeons finished amputating: "At the foot of a tree, within ten yards of the front of the house, I notice a heap of amputated feet, legs, arms, hands . . ."

Amputated body parts were buried in pits near the hospitals.

through the skin, fat, and muscle surrounding the bone. He left enough skin and muscle to cover the end of the amputated limb.

In rare cases, the damaged part (finger, toes, hands, feet, arms, or legs) could be successfully separated from the rest of the body at a joint. The surgeon cut the ligaments holding the bones together. But typically, the bone above or below the joint was sawed in half.

After the surgeon completed the amputation, he tied off severed blood vessels using surgical thread made of silk, cotton, or horsehair. Then he pulled the skin and muscle over the bone end and stitched it up.

It was a gory business. A Confederate nurse wrote in her journal about the many amputations performed in the hospital she served. "A stream of blood ran from the table into a tub in which was the arm. It had been taken off at the socket, and the hand, which but a short time before grasped the musket and battled for the right, was hanging over the edge of the tub, a lifeless thing."

A Union soldier observed the surgeons at work during the Battle of Chancellorsville. "As each amputation was completed the wounded man was carried to the old house and laid on the floor; the arm or leg was thrown on the ground near the table, only a few feet from the wounded who were laying near by."

Private J. W. Gibson, a thirty-five-year-old Confederate soldier from Missouri, was assigned to assist operating surgeons. If a patient struggled, Gibson's job was to hold him down. The amputations haunted the soldier. "One doctor carried a knife with a long thin blade," Gibson remembered. "He would draw this around the limb and cut the flesh to the bone. The second had a saw with which he sawed the bone. The third had a pair of forceps with which he clasped the blood vessels, and a needle with which he sewed the skin over the wound." Gibson thought they amputated too often. He informed the doctors, "I did not go to war to hold men while they butchered them."

SECOND OPINIONS

Gruesome accounts by soldiers who witnessed amputations made their way back to families and hometown newspapers through letters. Military surgeons, in both the North and the South, were accused of being butchers.

Medical director Jonathan Letterman acknowledged that a few surgeons had been incompetent. But he supported the majority of them, "a body of men who have labored faithfully and well." Rather than acting as butchers, he wrote, "I am convinced that if any fault was committed it was that the knife was not used enough."

His view was shared by numerous doctors caring for men who had not been amputated and whose wounds led to infection and death. A Confederate surgeon later said that the southern doctors performed only as many surgeries as were necessary. Their concern was "first, as to the life of the wounded soldier, secondly, as to his future comfort and usefulness."

Still, the public criticisms led the Union and Confederate medical departments to impose regulations that prevented inept surgeons from performing unwarranted amputations. For each case, especially when

GENERAL DANIEL SICKLES
(1819–1914)

During the Battle of Gettysburg, Union general Daniel Sickles was hit by a cannonball as he rode his horse. The damage to his lower right leg was so severe that a field hospital surgeon amputated. Using crutches to get around, Sickles remained in the army, but he did not participate in combat. In this photograph taken after his amputation, Sickles (left) meets with Union general Samuel Heintzelman.

Sickles donated his severed leg to the Army Medical Museum at the surgeon general's office in Washington. On the anniversary of his amputation, he liked to visit the museum to see it. The cannonball next to the leg bone is the same kind that hit Sickles.

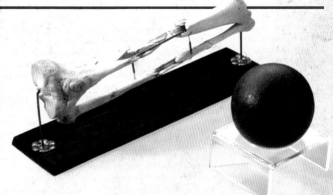

there was some doubt, the experienced surgeons at a hospital consulted to decide whether amputation was the best option. The most skilled surgeon performed the operation.

Even if a surgeon realized an amputation was the best way to save a man's life, it was a difficult decision. After an 1864 battle in Arkansas, one Confederate surgeon wrote in his diary: "All day long until late in the evening I was operating, taking off arms and legs and whatever else was needed to be done. I never took off so many in one day before [I'm] sorry that it was necessary to remove so many."

Survival rates from operations improved as surgeons gained more experience and the incompetent doctors were weeded out. A soldier's chance of coming through alive was better than in the Crimean War in Europe a few years earlier.

Field hospitals were intended to be temporary. As soon as possible, the wounded were transported away from the battlefield to hospitals in larger towns and cities for recovery. The severely injured, such as those with leg fractures or amputations, couldn't be moved by ambulance or train without causing more damage. They remained at the field hospitals, sometimes for weeks.

But even if a man survived a battlefield wound and the surgery, he wasn't out of the woods yet. Grave peril lay ahead. Infection.

Surgeons saved many lives at the field hospitals. The patients who died were buried close by. These men dig graves for dead soldiers at a Fredericksburg field hospital in May 1864.

I n May 1861, Allison Shutter, age fifteen, signed up as a drummer boy in a Pennsylvania regiment. A year later, during one of the battles on the Virginia Peninsula, pieces of an artillery shell struck Shutter in the knee. Unable to run, he was captured. A southern surgeon performed an excision at a Confederate field hospital. Union troops moved in soon after, rescuing Shutter. The photograph, showing his scar, was taken a few months later at a Union military hospital. Shutter was discharged from the army about seven months after his surgery, with partial use of his leg.

R ichard Dunphy, an Irish immigrant, was in his early-twenties when he enlisted in the U.S. Navy in 1863. As a coal heaver, his job was to shovel and haul the fuel that kept the ship's steam engines running. During the August 1864 Battle of Mobile Bay, Alabama, Dunphy was wounded by metal pieces of exploding artillery shells. Surgeons had to amputate both arms.

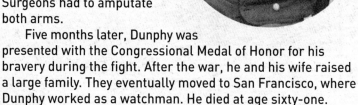

Five months later, Dunphy was presented with the Congressional Medal of Honor for his bravery during the fight. After the war, he and his wife raised a large family. They eventually moved to San Francisco, where Dunphy worked as a watchman. He died at age sixty-one.

W hen Robert Fryer enlisted in a New York regiment in 1864, he claimed to be a farmer, age eighteen. He was actually a year younger. Seven months later, Fryer was wounded in Virginia. Surgeons removed three fingers from his right hand. His thumb and forefinger continued to move normally. This photograph was taken before he left a Washington hospital for home. Fryer became a minister and settled in Indiana. He died of a stroke in 1918.

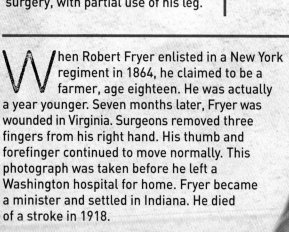

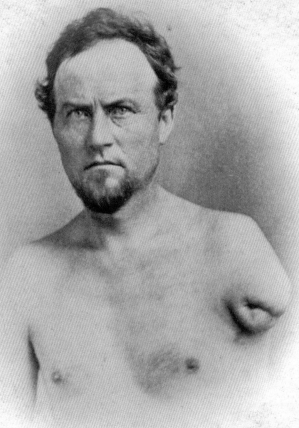

Edward Estell was forty-four and married with several children when he joined the U.S. Army in September 1864. At the Battle of Petersburg in early April 1865, Estell was shot in the left arm. Surgeons at the field hospital amputated. After three days, he was transferred to Washington, where he recovered. Discharged in July, Estell returned to his family in Pennsylvania and ultimately had three more children. He couldn't wear an artificial arm because his amputation was too close to the shoulder joint. Estell died thirteen years after his injury.

Martin Restle, a German immigrant, had enlisted in the U.S. Army before the Civil War broke out. His regiment remained on the West Coast during the war. When Restle's enlistment ended in 1863, he returned to New York. The next year, the twenty-seven-year-old signed up in a New York regiment as a substitute for another man who paid Restle to serve. This was allowed in the North after the 1863 draft began.

On April 2, 1865, just as the war was winding down, Restle was shot in the lower leg during battle. The Minié ball caused so much damage that the leg had to be immediately amputated at a Virginia field hospital. Following his surgery, Restle was transferred to Washington, where he recuperated in a general hospital. This photograph was taken during his recovery. After the war, Restle lived for a time at a government home for disabled soldiers in Maine.

WALT WHITMAN
(1819–1892)

In December 1862, forty-three-year-old writer Walt Whitman spotted the name of his younger brother George on a list of casualties from the Battle of Fredericksburg. He left his home in Brooklyn, New York, and traveled to Virginia to find him. Fortunately, George had only received a slight facial wound from an exploding artillery shell.

Relieved, Whitman decided to stay and help care for hundreds of seriously injured men at the Lacy House field hospital. From there, he traveled to Washington where he volunteered in the capital's hospitals. Whitman bought sweet treats and other food and gifts for patients. He wrote letters for them, read to them, and kept them company. Later, Whitman created poetry and prose about his Civil War hospital experiences, including *Drum-Taps* and *Memoranda during the War*.

CLARA BARTON
(1821–1912)

Clara Barton, from Massachusetts, was a clerk at the U.S. Patent Office when the Civil War broke out. In a speech, she later explained why she volunteered: "I was strong—and I thought—I ought to go to the rescue of the men who fell."

Throughout the war, Barton operated independently of the commissions or the U.S. Army. She organized donations of clothing, food, and bandages and had them delivered to Union soldiers. Traveling to battlefields and hospitals, she helped the soldiers in any way she could, nursing them and providing comfort. After observing her in action, one Union surgeon called her the "angel of the battlefield."

With a fight expected at Fredericksburg in early December 1862, Barton headed there to offer her assistance. Like Walt Whitman, she worked at the Lacy House field hospital after the battle. The wounded filled the building, lying on every inch of open space. So much blood covered the wooden floors that her dress hem was soaked. She ignored it and continued attending to the wounded. The condition of the men and the hospital upset her. "The surgeons do *all* they *can*," she wrote in her journal, "but no provision had been made for such a wholesale slaughter on the part of any one."

Beginning in March 1865, Barton operated the Missing Soldiers Office to help families of Union soldiers find their loved ones. The chaos of a battle and its aftermath caused records of the dead to be incomplete. Sometimes no one, including the soldier's commander, wrote a family to inform them of a man's fate. Barton's office was asked to locate tens of thousands of soldiers. She and her staff discovered what had happened to about 22,000 of them. Nearly four years after the war ended, Barton believed that as many as 40,000 soldiers were still unaccounted for.

In 1881, Barton founded the American Red Cross, a volunteer organization. The Red Cross aids people affected by natural disasters, wars, and other emergencies by providing medical care, food, and shelter.

CHAPTER TEN

PUS
AND
GANGRENE

"During the Civil War I cannot recall
a single wound that was not infected."
—*W. W. Keen, Union surgeon*

Lieutenant Nathaniel Austin was shot on the final day of the Battle of Gettysburg. More than half of his South Carolina regiment was killed, wounded, or captured during the battle. Austin, in his early thirties, received a bullet to his chest that broke his right collarbone and shoulder blade. He was captured by the Union army and taken to a field hospital.

Two weeks after his injury, an infection developed on Austin's right arm. Within a few days, the arm was discolored and swollen, and a surgeon cut into it to release pus. About two weeks later, the infection had reached Austin's right hip and shoulder. The tonics, wet bandages, and iodine applied to the infected areas had little effect. Seven weeks after he'd been shot, Austin was dead.

MALIGNANT PUS

During a raging battle, Civil War surgeons paid little attention to the cleanliness of their hands, their surgical instruments, or the wounded man's skin. While patients recovered in the hospital, bandages and dressings were often used on more than one soldier—without sterilizing. Doctors, nurses, and attendants touched areas around open wounds with unwashed hands. As a result, an infected wound—even a minor one—was the rule, not the exception.

Wounds almost always formed pus. Surgeons called one kind laudable pus. When a patient had this creamy discharge, doctors were encouraged. In their view, this meant that the wound would heal without killing the man. Pus, we now know, is a sign of infection and is a mix of bacteria, white blood cells, and dead tissue.

The other kind was called malignant pus. The thinner, bloody, foul-smelling discharge was a sign to Civil War doctors that the infection would probably spread and lead to deadly blood poisoning.

According to medical ideas at the time, infections came from miasma. Doctors didn't realize that microbes were to blame. Today, medical historians believe that laudable pus was a sign of mild infection caused by *Staphylococcus* bacteria. Malignant pus, however, indicated a more serious

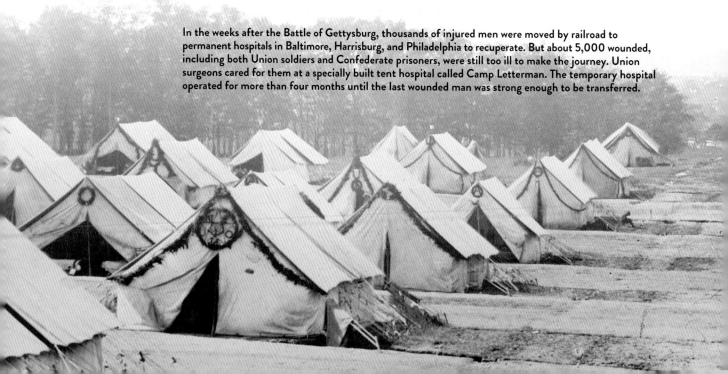

In the weeks after the Battle of Gettysburg, thousands of injured men were moved by railroad to permanent hospitals in Baltimore, Harrisburg, and Philadelphia to recuperate. But about 5,000 wounded, including both Union soldiers and Confederate prisoners, were still too ill to make the journey. Union surgeons cared for them at a specially built tent hospital called Camp Letterman. The temporary hospital operated for more than four months until the last wounded man was strong enough to be transferred.

infection caused by *Streptococcus* bacteria. In the 1860s, antibiotics to kill these bacteria hadn't yet been discovered.

LETHAL INFECTIONS

A patient recovering from a wound or surgery faced the risk of contracting dangerous bacterial infections, such as erysipelas, hospital gangrene, and tetanus.

Erysipelas started with a break in the skin as small as a scratch that allowed in streptococcal bacteria. As the infection spread deeper, the skin became red and sore. Victims frequently ran high fevers. If the bacteria reached the bloodstream, they traveled through the body, damaging organs and killing the patient. Victims of erysipelas, such as Lieutenant Nathaniel Austin, died in 40 percent of the recorded Civil War cases.

Hospital gangrene was a bacterial infection that caused tissue around a wound to die and rot. The condition gained its name because it was most common in large military hospitals. The flesh around even a minor skin wound was destroyed at an alarming rate. The damage often expanded at a half an inch an hour—or faster. The wound reeked. Hospital gangrene reached other parts of the body through the bloodstream. The infection came on suddenly, and a patient could be dead in less than a day.

Surgeons tried to stop its spread by removing the dead tissue and cleaning the wound with bromine, nitric acid, iodine, or carbolic acid. This was so painful that patients were usually first anesthetized with chloroform. In many cases, the treatment worked. What doctors didn't know then was that these chemicals killed the infection-causing microbes. Surgeons sometimes resorted to amputating limbs to cut off the gangrenous area. Despite their efforts, about half of hospital gangrene patients died.

Because hospital gangrene is now rare, some medical experts think it may have been caused by types of streptococcal bacteria more lethal than those we see today.

As the war continued, doctors observed that erysipelas and hospital gangrene spread from patient to patient and from patient to nurse. In their (faulty) view, poisonous fumes emanated from diseased people and rotting

ERYSIPELAS

George Lincoln of Illinois, age twenty-seven, was wounded in February 1862 at the Battle of Fort Donelson, Tennessee. A bullet tore through his foot, smashing the bones. Ten days after his injury, a Union surgeon amputated Lincoln's foot at a Nashville hospital. Soon after, the signs of erysipelas appeared on the amputated stump. The infection spread through his body, killing the soldier within the week.

material. When the contaminated air reached another person's body, it caused infection.

To prevent that, hospitals isolated victims in tents away from other patients. Tents allowed air to circulate, and the doctors thought this prevented the accumulation of harmful miasmas.

At the same time, nurses and attendants were careful not to use sponges, sheets, or bandages from erysipelas and hospital gangrene patients on others.

The medical staff sprayed chemicals such as bromine in a hospital ward. They poured disinfectants (chlorine, carbolic acid, iodine, and bromine) over body waste, including feces, vomit, and wound pus. They also used these chemicals to clean latrines and bedpans.

This wasn't done to kill microbes. Instead, the medical community believed the chemicals purified the air by neutralizing poisons given off by the foul-smelling substances.

Separation of contagious patients, strict hygiene, and disinfectant chemicals *did* control the spread of infections, but not for the reasons Civil War doctors thought. Isolation and cleanliness stopped the bacteria's transmission, and disinfectants destroyed them. And by the end of the war, fewer soldiers developed and died from these infections.

LOCKJAW

Another fatal wound complication was tetanus, or lockjaw. This infection is caused by a bacterium found in manure or in soil containing animal feces. When the bacteria enter a deep wound, they release toxins. The poisons cause painful muscle spasms so powerful that they can break bones. The jaw clenches shut. Muscles all over the body painfully cramp. Back muscles bend the spine into a backward arch. Patients can't swallow or breathe easily, and most die within several days of the symptoms' onset.

Wounded soldiers were at risk when exposed to animal manure in barns serving as field hospitals. Men with open wounds also developed tetanus after lying in muddy farm fields for days before they were rescued.

Civil War doctors thought tetanus resulted from "excessive heat, exposure to cold and damp air" and the improper cleaning of wounds. They blamed the muscle spasms on nerve damage caused by the pressure of bullets, bone splinters, and probing surgeon fingers.

The doctors were right about the inadequate cleaning. Foreign objects in the wound caused the disease if they were contaminated with tetanus bacteria. Although surgeons typically washed away dirt, they weren't able to remove the lingering bacteria deep in a wound.

Once a patient developed tetanus, there was no effective treatment. Some surgeons amputated limbs above the wound hoping to stop the infection from spreading to the entire body. Today, people are vaccinated to prevent this disease. But during the Civil War, there was no such vaccine. Nine of ten infected soldiers died an agonizing death.

TETANUS

Alexander Fletcher of Maine was twenty-one when he was shot in the arm and side at the Battle of the Wilderness. After treatment in a Virginia field hospital, Fletcher was moved to a general hospital in Washington.

Two weeks after his injury, symptoms of tetanus appeared. Doctors gave Fletcher painkillers and sedatives to help him sleep, providing a bit of relief. But he died about four weeks after his injury.

Surgeons performed an autopsy on Fletcher's body, hoping to learn what killed him. They discovered that when he was shot, the bullet (likely contaminated with tetanus bacteria) had lodged in the bone of his upper leg. Before the discovery of X-rays, doctors had no way to see a bullet far inside a wounded person's body.

An 1865 illustration of a soldier suffering from the intense muscle spasms of tetanus.

Infections caused the deaths of many Union and Confederate soldiers. But others survived their injuries and healed, thanks to innovations in hospital care and the contributions of countless woman volunteers.

HOSPITAL GANGRENE

John Parmenter signed up with a Pennsylvania volunteer regiment when he was sixteen. After only a few months as a soldier, he was shot in the ankle by a Minié ball during one of the war's last battles, in April 1865. The wound didn't heal, and within two weeks, it was gangrenous. This photograph (top) shows Parmenter's infected foot. It was taken in June 1865 at Harewood Hospital in Washington.

Despite doctors' attempts to stop gangrene's spread, the infection destroyed Parmenter's skin and bone. He grew weaker by the day. To save his life, his surgeon amputated the lower third of Parmenter's leg (right). According to medical records, the remaining stump healed well enough for doctors to release the teen from the hospital a month after his surgery.

Isadore Wick, around age thirty, enlisted with a New York City regiment in August 1861. At the Battle of Fredericksburg, December 1862, a Minié ball shattered his lower leg. A field hospital surgeon amputated it.

About two weeks later, Wick was transferred to a Washington hospital. Unfortunately, it was a hospital known for its careless attendants, bad odors, and failure to change bandages often enough. Near Wick's bed, another soldier developed hospital gangrene. Not long after, the open wound on Wick's amputated stump showed the signs of infection—rotting skin and a nauseating odor. He was moved to a separate ward for hospital gangrene patients.

Soon Wick developed diarrhea. His pulse raced. He was pale and weak. The doctor prescribed food, tonics, and opium, but they had no effect. Nitric acid applied to the damaged skin didn't stop the infection's advance. The end of the amputated stump turned black. His health rapidly declining, Wick became delirious.

Four months after his injury, and after much suffering, Isadore Wick died.

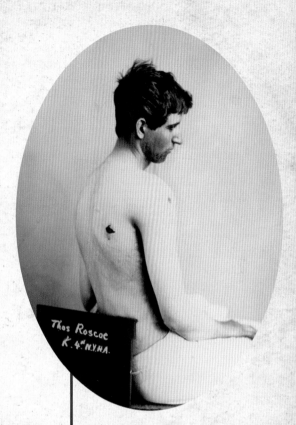

Thomas Roscoe was nineteen when he enlisted in a New York artillery regiment in late 1863, serving alongside his older brother. In early April 1865, Roscoe was shot in the shoulder. After three days, he was moved from a Virginia field hospital to a large Washington hospital, where this photograph was taken. His wound refused to heal, and it became gangrenous. Doctors couldn't help him. Roscoe failed quickly, dying less than three weeks after his injury.

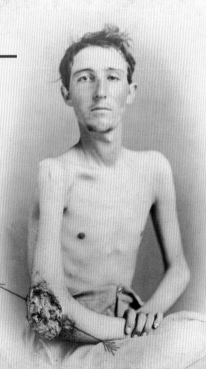

In March 1865, New Yorker James Stokes, age twenty, was shot by a Minié ball in the elbow. The red arrow shows the bullet's path. His wound was slowly healing when it developed hospital gangrene. Doctors treated it successfully with turpentine and kerosene, though the damaged joint had reduced motion. Stokes survived the war, later working as a farmer and a hotel keeper. He died in 1905 at age sixty.

The U.S. Capitol as a Union hospital in 1862. The women in the scene are volunteers who read to wounded soldiers, wrote letters for them, and nursed them. Other nurses were male soldiers. During the war, about 2,000 soldiers were patients at the Capitol.

1862

HEALING

> "The vivid recollections of what I have witnessed
> during years of horror have been so shocking,
> that I have almost doubted whether
> the past was not all a fevered dream, and, if real,
> how I ever lived through it."
>
> —KATE CUMMING, CONFEDERATE HOSPITAL MATRON

In November 1862, Private Rice Bull's boyhood friend—and fellow soldier—fell critically ill with typhoid fever. The surgeon of their New York regiment sent the sick man to a nearby Union hospital for care. After Bull, age twenty, heard that his friend was not improving, he got permission from his commanding officer to visit.

The hospital was located in an abandoned cotton mill in western Virginia. It only treated soldiers with disease, including typhoid fever, malaria, and dysentery. Each of the building's several stories contained a ward with two hundred cots. One ward was set aside for patients whom doctors expected to die. That was where Bull found his friend, who, in addition to typhoid, had developed gangrene in both feet. Surgeons had already amputated some of his toes.

Bull watched as other sick soldiers arrived at the hospital from their regiments. Nurses and attendants washed them, took their dirty clothes, and gave them clean underwear. The hospital workers (of which there were too few) were other soldiers who knew nothing about nursing. Most didn't want to learn. Bull was dismayed by what he saw, and he devoted himself to helping his friend recover.

The armies refitted passenger and freight cars to carry the wounded by train from field hospitals to general hospitals in the cities. A patient's bumpy journey lying on the car floors was often cushioned only by straw. Confederate trains and tracks deteriorated as the war went on, and rides in the trains were excruciating. Some Union trains, like this one, were designed with bunks that supported stretchers. Sturdy rubber bands absorbed the train's motion, sparing the wounded the painful jolts. This drawing appeared in the February 27, 1864 issue of *Harper's Weekly*.

With Bull's care, the young man eventually was well enough to be discharged from the army and sent home. Impressed by the way Bull nursed his friend, one of the surgeons asked him to stay on as an attendant.

"Nothing could have induced me to continue in that work," Bull wrote in his diary. "This had been my first experience in the horrors of war as shown by our terrible Hospital Service."

GENERAL HOSPITALS

Before the war, most Americans had never seen the inside of a hospital. You were born and died in your home. If you felt ill, a family member—usually a woman—cared for you. The few hospitals were in big cities and generally for people who had no homes, money, or anyone to help them. Nursing care in public hospitals was provided by servants or by recovering patients. There were no professional nurses in the United States.

When the war started, the military set up hospitals in houses, schools, hotels, churches, warehouses, and government buildings. In Washington, even the Capitol was used. Both armies were reluctant to construct new, expensive buildings.

The *Red Rover* was a Confederate steamboat captured by the Union on the Mississippi River in April 1862. The U.S. Army turned it into a floating hospital, using money donated by the Western Sanitary Commission. Other hospital boats, including many supplied by sanitary commissions, carried the sick and wounded from temporary hospitals near the battlefield to permanent ones in cities. Boats were also used to quarantine smallpox patients.

These hospitals were often ghastly places. Mary Livermore of the U.S. Sanitary Commission described one in Cairo, Illinois, made up of several small houses and sheds. "The fetid odor of typhoid fever, erysipelas, dysentery, measles, and healing wounds," she wrote, "was rendered more nauseating by unclean beds and unwashed bodies."

LOUISA MAY ALCOTT
(1832–1888)

Alcott, from Massachusetts, was a writer who later gained fame for her books, including *Little Women*. In late 1862, she volunteered as a nurse at a Union hospital located in a former Washington hotel. After just a few weeks, Alcott contracted typhoid fever. Weakened and too sick to work, she was forced to return home. She never fully recovered her health.

Alcott wrote of her experiences in *Hospital Sketches*, published in 1863. In one section, she describes a day on a ward with forty patients: "I spent my shining hours washing faces, serving rations, giving medicine, and sitting in a very hard chair, with pneumonia on one side, diptheria [*sic*] on the other, five typhoids on the opposite, and a dozen dilapidated patriots, hopping, lying, and lounging about."

Nurses, volunteers, and visitors struggled with the smell of rotting flesh, urine, and feces. Louisa May Alcott recalled: "The first thing I met was a regiment of the vilest odors that ever assaulted the human nose." To mask the stench, she sprinkled cologne on herself. A volunteer Confederate nurse in Richmond carried bottles of smelling salts and camphor in her pocket to sniff when the "sickening, dead odor" in the hospital grew overpowering.

As the number of wounded and sick soldiers skyrocketed, existing hospital buildings became too crowded. Armies put up large tents, which had the advantage of good ventilation. But that didn't solve the problem. More and more soldiers needed long-term care. Union and Confederate officials realized that they had to build permanent hospitals.

Lincoln General Hospital, built in the pavilion style, was Washington's largest military hospital. It had enough beds for more than 2,500 patients. During its operation between December 1862 and August 1865, the hospital treated at least 25,000 soldiers.

The ward of a Union hospital in Washington, in 1864, shows the high ceilings, ample windows, and wide spacing between beds that provided good ventilation. Visitors sit with the patients. Medical staff change bandages and examine the bedridden. Several patients in the photograph are amputees. The garlands of greenery in the rafters added a pleasant scent from pines and other plants. This was thought to prevent poisonous miasma from infecting the hospital. The decoration also brightened up the wards.

Both armies used the pavilion style for their new hospitals. With this design, a hospital was laid out as several separate one-story buildings or wings. It allowed plenty of airflow, considered essential to preventing the buildup of toxic miasmas that came from patients' bodies. The wood structures could be erected quickly and expanded if casualties rose.

WHO WORKS THERE?

In the general hospitals of both the North and South, one surgeon was in charge. Each assistant surgeon was responsible for patients in one or two wards. The contract surgeons, who had less seniority, did similar work. Each hospital had a steward, and large facilities had several.

A ward was assigned its own nurses and attendants. The patients, frail and unable to care for themselves, needed to be washed and fed. Their clothes, bedding, and bandages had to be regularly changed. Most patient care was performed by male soldiers temporarily assigned to hospital duty. Many of them were recuperating from illness or injury and weren't yet strong enough for fighting or other military tasks.

The hospital's matrons acted as housekeepers, keeping the facility running smoothly and efficiently. These women were in charge of the laundry and bedding, and they made sure that patients received medicine and food the doctors ordered, doing the cooking themselves when necessary. At times, a matron stepped in as a nurse, washing patients and writing letters.

Other hospital workers included clerks to keep records and to place supply orders, cooks and bakers, laundresses, carpenters, guards, and attendants to aid nurses and doctors. Union hospitals hired free blacks for these jobs, including men and women who had recently escaped slavery.

When members of black regiments fell ill or were wounded, they were treated in separate hospitals for black soldiers. In many cases, these hospitals lacked sufficient doctors and staff. Union hospital inspectors criticized some of the facilities for failing to wash patients and bed linens. Death rates were usually higher than at nearby hospitals for white troops.

While the Union assigned soldiers as nurses and attendants, the Confederate army ultimately ran so short of manpower that it couldn't spare even feeble, unhealthy soldiers. By the second part of the war, the majority of southern military hospital workers were slaves and free blacks forced

Deaths occurred every day at military hospitals. Bodies were kept in a morgue, called the dead room or dead house, until burial. Most soldiers were buried close to the hospital. These Union graves are near City Point Hospital, Virginia (right). For a fee, embalmers prepared bodies to be shipped home to loved ones. A Union embalming surgeon (left) injects preserving liquid into a corpse to prevent it from decaying before arriving at its destination.

into hospital service. These men and women worked as nurses, cooks, laundresses, and laborers. They made up three of every four workers at Richmond's Chimborazo Hospital, the South's largest.

Chimborazo had 100 separate wards in buildings laid out in the pavilion style, with beds for nearly 4,000 patients. Even that wasn't adequate for all the soldiers who needed care.

In May 1864, a Confederate soldier was taken there with a bullet wound in his leg. Alexander Hunter found the hospital overcrowded with too few doctors and staff. He described its stench and his disgusting bed ("a bag half stuffed with sawdust, which is red and sticky . . ."). He had bad memories of the place: "The three days I spent in that hospital were the

SALLY TOMPKINS
(1833–1916)

Sally Tompkins, a member of a wealthy Virginia family, was twenty-seven years old when the war broke out. After the early battles, Confederate wounded swamped Richmond. Tompkins established a hospital of about two dozen beds in the home of Judge John Robertson, who donated it for that purpose when he fled the city. Along with several slaves and women from an Episcopal church, Tompkins cared for injured soldiers, using donations and her own money.

The Confederate government later took charge of private hospitals. But President Jefferson Davis made an exception for Tompkins's Robertson Hospital because the recovery rate was so high. One Confederate soldier called it "incomparably the best in Richmond." To get around the new regulation, Davis made Tompkins a captain in the Confederate army, and the military helped support the hospital. Soldiers treated there throughout the war's four years (totaling more than 1,300 men) called her Captain Sally.

most terrible of my life; with nothing to do but to fight away the bloated flies which clung to the wounded spots until they were mashed." Hunter's politically connected sister soon arrived to whisk him off to Sally Tompkins's small, well-regarded hospital. He felt fortunate to have escaped Chimborazo.

Despite the conditions in some hospitals and the hundreds of thousands of patients who required care, a remarkable number of hospitalized soldiers recovered and survived the war.

A ROLE FOR WOMEN

Military leaders, doctors, and many in the public believed that army hospitals were too gruesome for women. But with such overwhelming numbers of sick and wounded soldiers, more nurses were desperately needed.

Dorothea Dix, who had worked to establish hospitals for the mentally ill, persuaded the U.S. War Department to allow her to supply trained woman nurses. In late spring 1861, the army made her Superintendent of Female Nurses. Dix had observed Florence Nightingale's approach to patient care during the Crimean War, and she promoted it with her nurses. Throughout the war, hundreds of Dix-appointed women were paid to serve in Union hospitals.

Military officers on both sides asked for nursing help from Catholic nuns. Since the 1840s, nuns had run charity hospitals and offered care during epidemics. Several hundred sisters from about a dozen different nun orders served at Union and Confederate hospitals, camps, and prisons.

Motivated by a strong desire to help the men from their communities, thousands of other women in the North and South came forward, too. They had experience nursing their families. They knew which foods and drinks aided recovery. They were the ones who carried out the family doctor's medical instructions.

Florence Nightingale (1820–1910) was known for her work during the Crimean War. She successfully nursed soldiers back to health by maintaining clean hospital wards, clothing, and bedding. She made sure that the patients were bathed regularly and fed nourishing meals. In 1860, Nightingale started a school dedicated to training nurses, the first in the world. Her approach to patient care inspired women in both the North and South to volunteer as nurses.

DOROTHEA DIX (1802–1887)

Dorothea Dix was born in what is now Maine, spending her teen years in the Boston area. As a young woman, she was a teacher. Later she campaigned to help people who were considered insane from being neglected in jails and poorhouses. Dix helped to establish more than thirty hospitals for the mentally ill.

She was almost sixty when she organized the army nursing corps. Dix had particular standards for her trained nurses. They had to be between ages thirty and fifty and plainly dressed so that soldiers saw them as mothers, not girlfriends. She also appointed matrons, cooks, and laundresses to work for the U.S. Army.

Dix was more interested in ensuring that soldiers received good care than she was in making friends within the medical department. She never hesitated to criticize surgeons and army officers when she saw fault. As a result, Dix alienated many of them. "She was a stern woman of few words," recalled one of her nurses.

Amputees pose at the Armory Square Hospital in Washington, where they were receiving care and learning how to adapt to their disability.

Union records show that the U.S. Army hired at least 21,000 women to serve in military hospitals as nurses, matrons, laundresses, and cooks. More than 400 were black women acting as nurses. The count doesn't include unpaid volunteers and nuns. The sanitary commissions also hired female nurses.

In the South, where most battles occurred, women took soldiers into their homes and nursed them. Others, like Sally Tompkins, opened their own hospitals. The Confederates didn't have an organized system of training like Dorothea Dix's nursing corps. Although unpaid female volunteers pitched in, most southern army hospital nurses were male soldiers or slaves. Matrons, women who often performed nursing duties, were paid by the Confederate army. Because the official Confederate medical records burned in the Richmond fire, no one knows the exact number of southern women who served.

A soldier's chances of surviving his illness or wound depended on the quality of his hospital care. Women

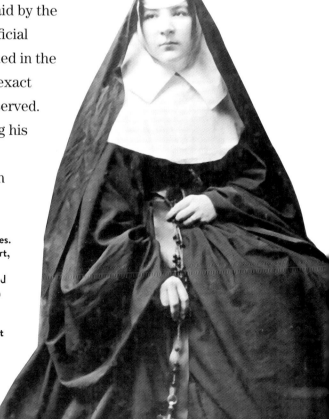

Nuns provided experienced nursing to both armies. This woman served at a Union hospital in Beaufort, South Carolina. One Virginia soldier praised the nuns in the Confederate hospitals and on the field after battles. "Blessings upon the sisterhood with its white caps, saintly presence, meek, soft eyes and tender touch; every veteran of the Army of Northern Virginia will always hold them in a most sweet remembrance."

filled a key role in this healing. They were generally seen as better able and more willing to help patients recover than the male soldiers who served as nurses.

Nursing eventually developed into a respectable female profession. This was one of the important ways the Civil War influenced American medical care during the years after the fighting ended.

This 1865 print was dedicated to the Union women who came to the aid and comfort of the soldiers. The scene shows members of the Ladies Aid Association as they help at a field hospital tent. A woman brings food in a basket. One writes a letter and reads to a wounded soldier. Another offers hot soup.

MOTHER BICKERDYKE
(1817–1901)

When the war began, Mary Ann Bickerdyke was a forty-four-year-old widow living in Illinois. She volunteered to take supplies from her town to a Union army camp in Cairo, Illinois, where many soldiers were sick with typhoid, measles, and respiratory illnesses. Appalled by the filthy military hospitals, Bickerdyke made it her business to clean them up.

Working with the U.S. Sanitary Commission, she set up laundries and kitchens at dozens of field hospitals. After battles, Bickerdyke helped rescue the wounded and prepared hospital boats on the Mississippi to evacuate them. She followed the army as it fought battles in Vicksburg and Atlanta, nursing the sick and injured. Grateful soldiers called her Mother Bickerdyke.

Bickerdyke wasn't intimidated by doctors or generals. In one case, when a surgeon arrived late at a hospital ward, she turned on him. "You miserable, drunken, heartless scalawag!" she cried. "What do you mean by leaving these fainting, suffering men to go until noon with nothing to eat, and no attention?" She reported him to the hospital's medical director, who fired the man.

The surgeon complained to General William Sherman that he'd been falsely accused. When Sherman heard that Bickerdyke had made the charges, he replied, "If it was she, I can't help you. She has more power than I—she ranks me."

SUSIE KING TAYLOR
(1848–1912)

Susie King Taylor was born a slave on an island off the Georgia coast. When she was seven, her owner sent her to live with her grandmother, a free black, in Savannah. Her grandmother arranged for her to learn to read and write—secretly, because it was against Georgia law for African Americans to be educated.

In April 1862, the Union navy took control of islands off the coast. Taylor and her family fled there for protection from the Confederates. Discovering that the young teen could read, Union officers asked her to run a school, teaching former slave children and adults.

That October, the family moved to Beaufort, on the South Carolina coast. Several relatives, including Taylor's new husband, joined a black Union regiment. She served as one of its laundresses. Taylor stayed with the regiment throughout the war, nursing sick and injured, teaching soldiers to read and write, and cleaning guns. She was never paid for her work. Taylor was one of hundreds of African American women—free blacks and former slaves—who supported black regiments by cooking, washing, and nursing.

After the war, Taylor moved to Boston. Nearly forty years later, she wrote a memoir about her experiences. Her goal, she said, was to show the role women played in the war: "[women] who did not fear shell or shot, who cared for the sick and dying; women who camped and fared as the boys did, and who are still caring for the comrades in their declining years."

KATE CUMMING
(CA. 1830–1909)

Born in Scotland, Kate Cumming settled with her family in Alabama more than ten years before the war began. After the South seceded, she volunteered to nurse soldiers at Confederate military hospitals. Her only experience was within her family, but Cumming quickly learned how to care for ill and wounded men.

In April 1862, she and a group of women traveled to Corinth, Mississippi, to help the injured brought there from the Battle of Shiloh, Tennessee. For the rest of the war, Cumming worked in hospitals of the Confederate Army of Tennessee as a matron. She managed the wards and kitchens and cared for patients.

Cumming kept a journal, which she published in 1866. In one entry from May 1862, she expressed her thoughts about nursing the soldiers: "A number of men, wounded in a skirmish, have been brought in to-day. . . . We wash their hands and faces, which is a great treat to them, as they are covered with dust; we bathe their wounds, which are always inflamed, and give them something refreshing to drink. O, I do feel so glad that I am here, where I can be of some little service to the poor fellows."

AFTER
THE
GUNS FELL
SILENT

"We did not do the best we would,
but the best we could."
—WILLIAM H. TAYLOR, CONFEDERATE SURGEON

B y June 1865, the last of the Rebel armies had surrendered. The U.S. Army captured the Confederacy's president, Jefferson Davis. The rebellion was over, and the union of the United States had been preserved. Slaves were free. Soldiers and sailors returned to their families.

THE POWS

Among the men who went home were prisoners of war. Several hundred thousand soldiers spent months and even years as captives. After the war ended and the prisoners were released, the public saw the full horror of the camps. Men emerged emaciated and deathly ill. Both Northerners and Southerners shouted accusations of mistreatment. The charges were impossible to deny.

Two large prisons camps, built in 1864, were particularly notorious. At Andersonville, Georgia, 45,000 Union troops suffered in stifling heat and wet cold. About 13,000 of them died.

In September 1864, Confederate Surgeon General Moore sent Dr. Joseph Jones to inspect the prison. The southern physician reported that conditions were atrocious. Union prisoners suffered from scurvy, diarrhea, dysentery, typhoid fever, and hospital gangrene. "Millions of flies swarmed over everything and covered the faces of the sleeping patients," Jones wrote, "and crawled down their open mouths and deposited their maggots in the gangrenous wounds of the living and in the mouths of the dead."

The infamous Confederate prison camp at Andersonville, Georgia. This photograph from August 1864 shows the tents of blankets and sticks constructed by the prisoners. The wooden structure in the middle of the photograph is the latrine. Streams of water flow in and out of the toilet area, creating conditions that spread intestinal diseases. After the war, the prison's superintendent, Captain Henry Wirz, was convicted in a United States military trial of the deaths of thousands of prisoners. In November 1865, he was hanged.

The Union prison in Elmira, New York, called Hellmira by the Rebels. Groups of Confederate prisoners line up for roll call among the tents in which they lived. Poor sanitation, overcrowding, and a frigid winter led to the deaths of about a quarter of the prisoners.

At the Union prison camp in Elmira, New York, about 12,000 Confederate prisoners endured the brutal, icy winter of 1864–65. A soldier's only protection from snow and below-zero temperatures was a makeshift wooden barrack or tent, neither adequately heated. The conditions were hard on Southerners not used to snow and frigid weather. Nearly 3,000 died, earning the prison the name Hellmira.

Confederate hospital matron Kate Cumming was bitter about their treatment. "We starved their prisoners!" she later wrote. "But who laid waste our corn and wheat fields? And did not we all starve? Have the southern men who were in northern prisons no tales to tell—of being frozen in their beds, and seeing their comrades freeze to death for want of proper clothing?"

Phoebe Pember, a Confederate matron at Richmond's Chimborazo Hospital, admitted that the Union soldiers held by the South were in terrible physical condition. Still, she blamed the Union army for its abuse of Rebel captives. "The Federal prisoners we had released were in many instances in a like state," she wrote in her memoirs, "but our ports had been blockaded, our harvest burned, our cattle stolen, our country wasted. Even had we felt the desire to succor, where could the wherewithal have been found?" She believed the U.S. Army "could have fed his prisoners upon milk and honey, and not have missed either."

Prisoners of war on both sides were fed poorly and suffered from malnutrition. Scurvy was common. With weakened bodies, the men became susceptible to other diseases. They developed respiratory infections such as colds, bronchitis, and pneumonia. Their ailments worsened with exposure to harsh weather.

Contagious illnesses, such as smallpox, spread in the crowded prison conditions. Sanitation was usually poor. Human waste was dumped into drinking water sources, infecting soldiers with typhoid fever, dysentery, and diarrhea. Neither army had enough doctors to treat all its prisoners.

At least 55,000 men died in military prisons. Many of the survivors never fully recovered their health after the ordeal.

INCOMPLETE BODIES

Although the fighting had ended, the war's damage was far from over for the wounded. Historians estimate that at least 45,000 survivors were amputees. Before the war, most of the men had used their bodies to make a living—as farmers, construction workers, manual laborers. Without an arm or leg, they could no longer perform those jobs.

While the war was still raging, inventors created more than a hundred different designs for artificial limbs. Depending on the model, the

Charles Lapham, from Vermont, was twenty-three when a cannonball hit his legs during an 1863 Maryland battle. Two days later, a surgeon amputated both. After about a year, Lapham received two artificial legs that worked so well that he could climb stairs. He went on to work in the U.S. Treasury Department for more than twenty years, until his death at age fifty-one.

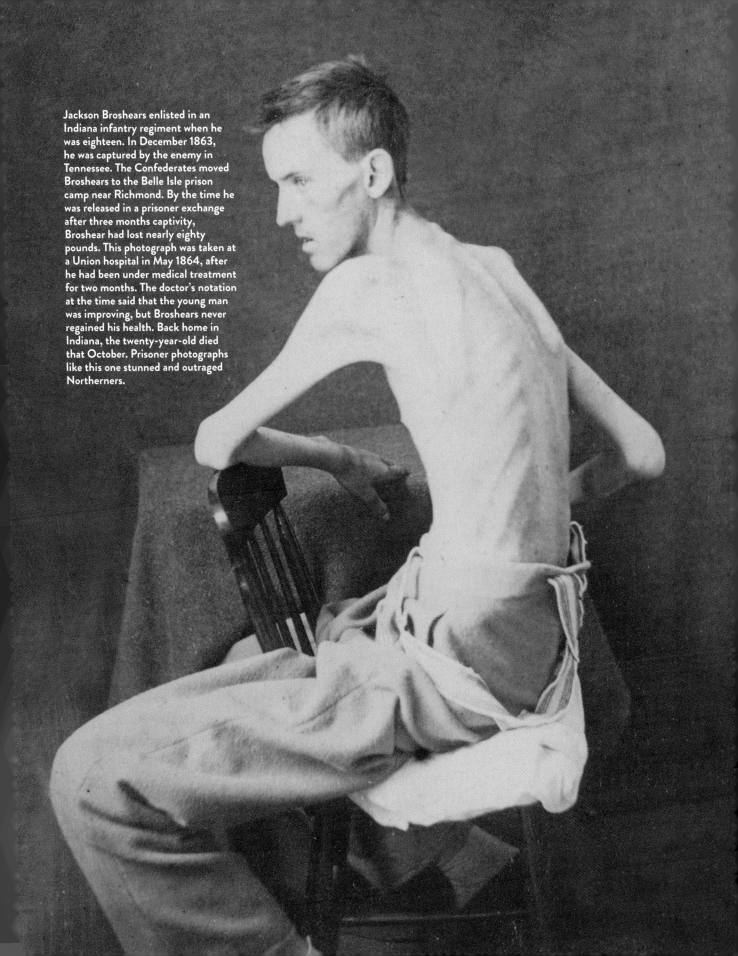

Jackson Broshears enlisted in an Indiana infantry regiment when he was eighteen. In December 1863, he was captured by the enemy in Tennessee. The Confederates moved Broshears to the Belle Isle prison camp near Richmond. By the time he was released in a prisoner exchange after three months captivity, Broshear had lost nearly eighty pounds. This photograph was taken at a Union hospital in May 1864, after he had been under medical treatment for two months. The doctor's notation at the time said that the young man was improving, but Broshears never regained his health. Back home in Indiana, the twenty-year-old died that October. Prisoner photographs like this one stunned and outraged Northerners.

prostheses were made of cork, wood, leather, rubber, metal, and cloth. The U.S. government paid for part of the cost of an amputee's artificial limb. But the benefit was strictly for Union soldiers, not Confederate veterans. Southern state governments and private charities helped Rebel amputees buy prostheses.

Many men learned to use their prosthetic limbs while recovering in the hospital. Special hospitals in the North taught wounded veterans new skills such as bookkeeping, telegraphing, and shoemaking. These jobs didn't require strenuous physical labor or full use of arms or legs.

With or without a prosthesis, though, many veterans were ashamed to be missing a limb.

In a June 1861 battle, Virginian James Hanger, age eighteen, was struck by a cannonball just two days after he enlisted. Hanger was captured, and a Union surgeon amputated his mangled leg.

After being released in a prisoner exchange two months later, Hanger went home to recover. He had been an engineering student before the war, and he decided to craft an artificial wooden leg for himself. The Hanger Limb worked so well that the young man convinced the Confederate government to buy it for other amputees. That was the beginning of the J. E. Hanger company, which still produces prosthetics today.

In this photograph from around 1902, an amputee wears an artificial leg made by the Hanger company.

Besides the amputees, tens of thousands of men—North and South—were left with some kind of disability. These included hearing loss from thundering artillery guns; joint damage from carrying heavy loads; and partial blindness from an eye injury. One soldier in a U.S. Colored Troops regiment tripped on a tree branch during a battle charge, and the other men unintentionally trampled him. His back was permanently damaged.

Union soldiers were eligible for government financial support. The amount they received depended on the extent of their disability and their military rank. Widows and orphans of dead soldiers could also get a pension. The system changed during the decades after the war, and starting in 1892, female Union nurses received pensions, too.

Confederate soldiers weren't eligible for these federal benefits. Each southern state eventually offered pensions to its veterans.

Many amputees used crutches and wheelchairs to get around. In some cases, men found prostheses uncomfortable. Others were unable to find a good fit. This soldier from Pennsylvania lost both his legs to amputation after an 1864 battle injury in Georgia.

SOLDIER'S HEART

War wounds weren't always as visible as a missing leg. The excitement and glory that soldiers expected to find in battle turned out to be terror and pain. They'd seen bullets and cannon shells tear human bodies apart. They'd watched friends suffer agonizing death from disease.

Long after they returned home, many men continued to be cursed with frightening memories and hallucinations of danger. In a physical reaction to these thoughts, their heart raced. Some abused alcohol or became violent. Their families noticed odd behavior and changes in personality.

At the time, this was called battle sickness, or soldier's heart. Today it is known as post-traumatic stress disorder (PTSD). In the 1800s, mental illnesses were not understood or treated the way they are now. Affected men sometimes committed suicide or ended up in mental hospitals suffering

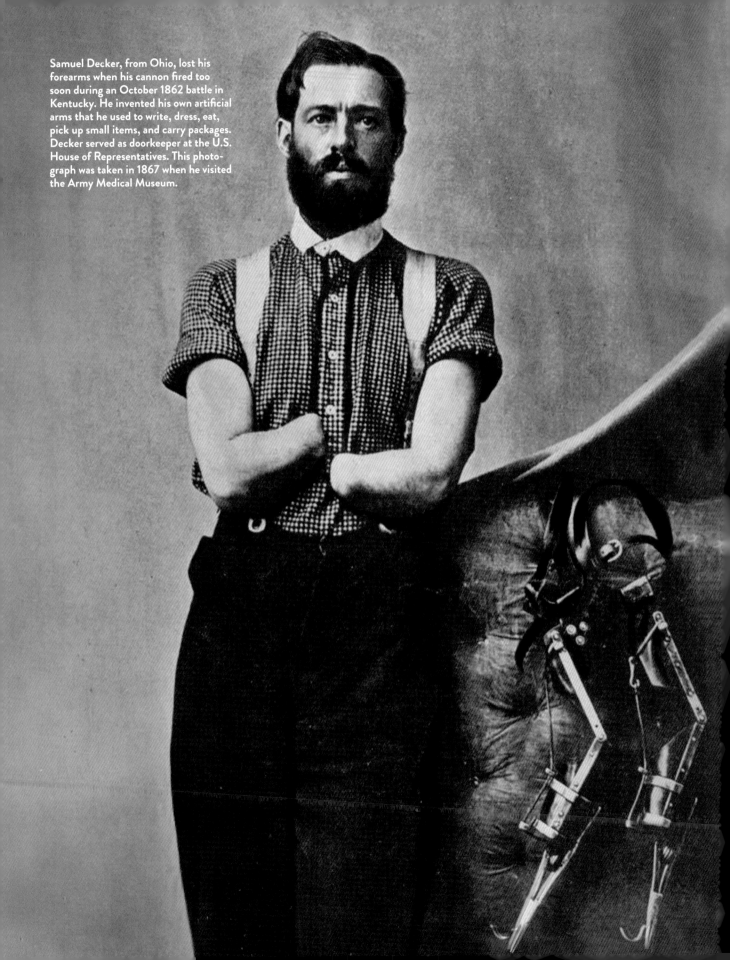

Samuel Decker, from Ohio, lost his forearms when his cannon fired too soon during an October 1862 battle in Kentucky. He invented his own artificial arms that he used to write, dress, eat, pick up small items, and carry packages. Decker served as doorkeeper at the U.S. House of Representatives. This photograph was taken in 1867 when he visited the Army Medical Museum.

from severe depression. Based on medical records of veterans seeking pensions, historians believe that these after-effects lasted longer and were more severe in soldiers who served as teens.

The conflict took a toll on the doctors, too. Union surgeon James Benton, from New York, wrote in a letter twenty years after fighting ended, "The war and three years of service have made me a physical wreck."

A SILVER LINING

The Civil War was a dreadful period of blood and germs. Because of the great number of casualties—unprecedented in American history—the medical community was forced to respond with improvisation, innovation, and education. From those terrible four years came changes that enhanced future medical care in the United States.

Physicians

Thousands of doctors went home with a deeper understanding of the human body and with more experience in diagnosing illnesses. They learned better ways to care for the sick and wounded. After performing countless operations, the surgeons developed skills which significantly improved by the war's end. Most of the surgeries were performed under anesthesia, demonstrating that chloroform and ether were effective and safe.

One Confederate physician wrote, "I have lost much, but I have gained much, especially as a medical man. I return home a better surgeon, a better doctor."

The American approach to medicine became more scientific. Encouraged by the army medical departments, doctors kept records of their treatments and surgical techniques. Then they shared what they'd learned with colleagues in order to improve recovery and survival rates. The sharing of knowledge continued after the war as new medical journals were published throughout the country.

In 1862, Union army Surgeon General William Hammond established the Army Medical Museum to collect specimens from surgeons, including bones from amputated limbs. The collection also contained photographs of injured soldiers, complete with information on their wounds and surgeries. The materials were intended as a resource for doctors who wanted to learn more about injuries, disease, and treatment. Starting in 1870, the war records were gathered together into the multivolume *Medical and Surgical History of the War of the Rebellion*, which became a valuable reference for physicians.

The Walker brothers of North Carolina enlisted together on the day their state seceded, May 20, 1861, around the time of this photograph. Levi (left) was nineteen, and Henry was twenty-four. Before the war began, they had worked alongside their father at a wool factory.

In July 1863, the Walkers were among more than 160,000 soldiers who fought at Gettysburg. On the battle's first day, Levi was shot while carrying his regiment's flag. A Confederate surgeon amputated his left leg the next day at a field hospital. When the southern army retreated two days later, Levi had to be left behind with about 7,000 other Confederate wounded. The Union army took him prisoner and held him for four months until his release in a prisoner exchange.

Henry, an officer, joined the rest of their regiment in the Confederate retreat from Gettysburg. About two weeks after his brother's injury, Henry was shot in the left leg in fighting at Hagerstown, Maryland. Just like his younger brother, he underwent an amputation. Henry, too, was taken prisoner, but he wasn't released for ten months.

Both brothers returned to North Carolina, married, and had children. Levi was a businessman, and Henry became a doctor. In 1887, the Walkers re-created the first photograph—without their left legs. They lived exceptionally long lives, with Levi dying at ninety-three and Henry at ninety-two.

Managing Casualties

Medical director Jonathan Letterman instituted a procedure to separate the wounded into three groups. That ensured that those who would most benefit from care received it first. This triage approach set the stage for our modern emergency response systems, both civilian and military.

An efficient system evolved to move the wounded from battlefield to hospital. Trained ambulance workers saved lives by speedily transporting the injured to doctors, just as emergency medical technicians (EMTs) and paramedics do today. New ambulance designs made the ride less jarring and painful to a wounded soldier.

Hospitals

Because so many ill and injured men had healed in military hospitals, public attitudes changed. Instead of considering a hospital as a place to die, Americans realized that it could be a place to recover. Hospitals assumed an important role in the nation's medical care. Doctors who had treated thousands of patients during the war managed these hospitals and served on the staffs.

Although no one yet understood that microbes caused diseases, the medical community had learned that lives were saved when hospital staffs used disinfectants and followed hygienic practices. Doctors observed that by isolating patients with contagious illnesses, such as smallpox and hospital gangrene, they could prevent epidemics.

Nursing

Women showed their value in healing the soldiers. Physicians recognized that hospitals were successful when they followed the same methods of care used by women for their families. Clean bodies, clothes, and bed linens. Nutritious food. Compassionate, personal attention. For the first time in the United States, nursing became a profession that women could pursue. In the years following the war, American schools devoted to nursing were founded.

Support For Veterans

Aid organizations were established early in the war to support the fighting men. When the war ended, these groups continued their mission. The U.S. Sanitary Commission helped soldiers receive back pay and pensions, showing them how to submit the correct forms to the appropriate government office. Relief groups assisted veterans in paying medical bills. They honored the soldiers' service by erecting monuments and maintaining cemeteries.

Union soldiers who lost limbs stand outside the office of the U.S. Christian Commission in Washington. Relief groups provided aid to soldiers whose injuries made it impossible to work.

This granite monument, crowned with a bald eagle, stands in a Burlington, Vermont, park. The state's chapter of the Woman's Relief Corps raised money to erect the monument in memory of Civil War soldiers and sailors, dedicating it on Memorial Day 1907.

Currier & Ives published this print in 1865. In memory of a loved one, people filled in the name of the dead soldier, his regiment, and where and when he died. Families often framed these memorials.

IN MEMORY OF

Ebenezer Bell

of the

88th Pa Reg Company

who died at

Laurel Hill Va

May the 5th 1864

A BRAVE AND GALLANT SOLDIER
AND A TRUE PATRIOT.

His toils are past, his work is done,
And he is fully blest.
He fought the fight, the victory won,
And enters into rest.

The blood and germs of the Civil War changed the lives of countless Americans. For many, the medical knowledge and experience gained during those four years offered hope for a healthier future. But for others, the legacy of the war was agony and loss. Even after the physical wounds healed, veterans and families couldn't escape the painful memories.

To honor those who died, some communities designated a day each spring when friends and loved ones gathered in tribute to the fallen. People placed flags and flowers on the graves, paraded through town, prayed, and gave speeches. This tradition spread across the country during the late nineteenth century, and it later expanded to honor Americans who died in subsequent wars. Today, Memorial Day is an official national holiday at the end of May.

Civil War remembrance events included the singing of old war songs. One of the most popular, "Tenting on the Old Camp Ground," expressed the sorrow that lingered for decades after the devastating conflict ended.

We are tired of war on the old camp ground,
Many are dead and gone,
Of the brave and true who've left their homes;
Others been wounded long.

We've been fighting today on the old camp ground,
Many are lying near;
Some are dead and some are dying,
Many are in tears.

(chorus)
Many are the hearts that are weary tonight,
Wishing for the war to cease;
Many are the hearts that are looking for the right,
To see the dawn of peace.
Tenting tonight, tenting tonight,
Tenting on the old camp ground.

TIMELINE

1853–56
Crimean War in Europe. Russia battles Turkey, Britain, and France.

1860
November 6
Abraham Lincoln elected president of the United States.

1861
February
Confederate States of America formed with Jefferson Davis as president.

March 4
Abraham Lincoln inaugurated as U.S. president.

April 12
Confederate troops fire on Ft. Sumter, SC, and Civil War begins.

April 29
Women's Central Association of Relief established in New York City.

June
Dorothea Dix appointed Superintendent of Nurses. U. S. Sanitary Commission established.

July 21
First Battle of Bull Run/ Manassas, VA.

July 30
Samuel Moore appointed Confederate surgeon general.

September 17
Battle of Antietam/ Sharpsburg, MD.

August 2
General George McClellan orders establishment of the ambulance corps for the Army of the Potomac.

June
Union hospital ship *Red Rover* begins service.

April 6–7
Battle of Shiloh, TN.

December 11–13
Battle of Fredericksburg, VA.
.

August 28–30
Second Battle of Bull Run/ Manassas, VA.

July
Jonathan Letterman takes over as medical director for the Army of the Potomac.

April 25
William Hammond appointed U.S. Army surgeon general.

March–July
Peninsula Campaign, VA; includes Battles of Fair Oaks/Seven Pines and Gaines's Mill.

February 12–16
Battle of Fort Donelson, TN.
1862

1863
January 1
Emancipation Proclamation goes into effect, freeing slaves in Confederate-held areas and allowing African Americans to join the U.S. military.

May 1–6
Battle of Chancellorsville, VA.

May
U.S. Colored Troops established.

May–July
Siege of Vicksburg, MS.

July 1–3
Battle of Gettysburg, PA.

September 18–20
Battle of Chickamauga, GA.

1864
February
Prison camp at Andersonville, GA, opens.

March 11
Congress establishes ambulance corps for the entire U.S. army.

May 5–7
Battle of the Wilderness, VA.

May 31–June 12
Battle of Cold Harbor, VA.

July
Prison camp at Elmira, NY, opens.

June–April 1865
Siege of Petersburg, VA.

August 5
Battle of Mobile Bay, Alabama

April 15
President Abraham Lincoln dies in Washington from an assassin's bullet.

April 9
General Robert E. Lee, head of the Confederacy's largest army, surrenders to Union general Ulysses S. Grant at Appomattox Court House, VA. By the end of May, the last Confederate army surrenders. The Civil War ends.

April 2–3
Confederate government evacuates Richmond; surgeon general's medical records burn in the fires that follow.
1865

November 8
Abraham Lincoln reelected U.S. president.

GLOSSARY

amputation: the surgical removal of part of the body.

anesthetic: a drug that stops a patient from feeling pain during surgery.

antibiotic: a drug used to destroy disease-causing bacteria.

artillery: large guns, such as cannons, that fire heavy balls or shells.

bacteria: microscopic one-celled organisms.

calomel: a medication containing mercury.

chloroform: an anesthetic used during Civil War surgeries.

Confederate (or Rebel) army: the military land forces of the Confederate States of America.

contagious disease: an illness that can be spread by contact with a person who has the disease.

diarrhea: an intestinal ailment in which bowel movements are watery and frequent.

dressing: material used to cover and protect a wound.

dysentery: an intestinal disease with symptoms of abdominal pain, vomiting, and severe, often bloody diarrhea.

epidemic: a disease that spreads to many members of a population at the same time.

erysipelas: an often fatal bacterial skin infection that spread in Civil War hospitals.

ether: an anesthetic used during Civil War surgeries. It was more flammable than chloroform.

excision (or resection): an alternative surgery to amputation in which only part of a damaged limb is removed.

feces: body waste discharged from the intestines.

germ theory: the idea that diseases can be caused by microorganisms.

hookworm: a blood-sucking parasite that lives in the small intestine and causes anemia, weakness, and abdominal pain.

hospital gangrene: death of body tissue caused by a bacterial infection.

hypothermia: the condition in which body temperature becomes too low from exposure to cold temperatures. Symptoms range from shivering to confusion to unconsciousness, organ failure, and death.

infectious disease: an illness caused by an organism such as a bacterium, virus, or parasite that invades the body.

latrine: the camp toilet.

laudanum: an opium-based medicine used to treat pain and a range of illnesses.

malaria: an infectious disease caused by parasitic microbes transmitted by mosquitoes. Symptoms include fever and chills.

matron: a woman who supervised overall housekeeping in hospitals.

measles: an extremely contagious disease caused by a virus. Symptoms include fever and red skin spots.

mercury: a toxic element that damages kidneys, brain, and nervous system. May also affect heart, lungs, and digestive system.

miasma: foul-smelling air coming from decomposing plant or animal material; once believed to cause disease.

microbe, or microorganism: a microscopic organism, such as a bacterium or virus.

Minié ball: a cone-shaped bullet.

morphine: an addictive drug derived from opium that induces sleep and dulls pain.

mumps: a disease caused by a virus with symptoms that include swollen glands, fever, muscle pain.

musket: a long-barreled gun carried by Civil War soldiers.

opium: an addictive drug made from the opium poppy that relieves pain and produces sleep.

parasite: an animal or plant that benefits from living in, with, or on another organism and often harms its host.

pest house: building where patients with contagious diseases were isolated from others.

pneumonia: lung infection with symptoms of cough, chest pain, rapid breathing, fever.

prosthesis: an artificial limb, such as an arm or leg.

pus: a thick fluid consisting of bacteria, white blood cells, and dead tissue formed during an infection.

quarantine: forced isolation to prevent the spread of a contagious disease.

quinine: a drug used to treat malaria.

regiment: an army group made up of about 1,000 soldiers. The size could be less, depending on the number of men who were recruited, sickened, captured, deserted, or killed.

scalpel: a small surgical knife used to cut through skin and other soft tissue.

scurvy: a disease caused by a lack of vitamin C. Symptoms include bleeding gums and extreme weakness.

secession: the withdrawal of southern states from the United States.

smallpox: a contagious, often fatal disease caused by a virus. Symptoms include high fever and skin sores.

steward: a surgical assistant in charge of preparing and dispensing medicines, among other hospital duties.

tapeworm: a parasitic worm that lives in the intestines.

tetanus: a disease in which muscles tighten involuntarily, caused by bacteria found in manure and soil that enter the body through deep cuts.

tourniquet: a device wrapped around an arm or leg and tightened to stop bleeding.

tuberculosis (consumption): a serious and sometimes fatal lung disease caused by a bacterium. Symptoms include cough, fever, chest pain, and weight loss.

typhoid fever: an infectious disease caused by a bacterium that spreads through food and water contaminated with body waste. Symptoms include high fever, headache, reddish skin spots, and bleeding from intestines.

typhus: an infectious disease caused by a bacterium that is transmitted by fleas, lice, mites, and ticks. Symptoms include severe headache, high fever, and red skin rash.

urine: body waste discharged from the kidneys.

Union (or Federal) army: the military land forces of the United States, called Yankees.

vaccine: a special preparation of killed or weakened microbes that triggers the body to produce immunity to a disease.

virus: a minute particle composed of a protein shell containing genetic material. It often causes disease when it invades living cells.

yellow fever: a disease caused by a virus and spread by mosquitoes. Symptoms include fever, vomiting, and body aches.

MORE
— TO —
EXPLORE

*Websites active at time of publication

PLACES TO VISIT IN PERSON AND ONLINE

National Museum of Civil War Medicine
Frederick, Maryland
civilwarmed.org

The museum offers exhibits about Civil War surgical care, medicines, doctors, nurses, soldiers' camp life, and more. The website provides many additional resources, such as podcasts, videos, digital exhibits, lectures, blog articles, photographs of artifacts, and other information about medicine during the Civil War.

civilwarmed.org/explore/primary-sources/

Here you can find primary sources, such as images, memoirs, letters, diaries, newspaper articles, and official reports. Topics include nurses, doctors, soldiers, the Sanitary Commission, Letterman's system, children of war, and African Americans in Civil War medicine.

youtube.com/user/nmcwm/videos

Watch short videos about medical equipment and techniques. Examples: how a tourniquet was used; the contents of a surgeon's amputation kit; the mystery of the mummified arm found at the Antietam battlefield.

Pry House Field Hospital Museum
Keedysville, Maryland, at the Antietam National Battlefield
civilwarmed.org/pry/

Part of the National Museum of Civil War Medicine, the Pry farm served as a Union field hospital during the battle of Antietam. Exhibits show how wounded soldiers received emergency medical care.

Clara Barton Missing Soldiers Office Museum
Washington, DC
clarabartonmuseum.org

Visit the museum and website to learn about Clara Barton's work with injured soldiers during the Civil War and about her later accomplishments.

The Exchange Hotel Civil War Medical Museum
Gordonsville, Virginia
hgiexchange.com

The hotel and nearby properties served as a short-term Confederate hospital on the railroad line to Richmond. About 70,000 patients were treated here during the war, both Confederate and Union soldiers. See surgical instruments and other medical equipment, stretchers, prosthetics, and a hospital room with cots.

National Park Service
nps.gov

The National Park Service maintains historical parks around the country related to the Civil War. Each offers exhibits and guided tours. Search by state at the main site. Two examples:

Richmond National Battlefield Park
Richmond, Virginia
nps.gov/rich/index.htm

The park includes multiple locations in the Confederacy's former capital and a medical museum on the site of the South's largest hospital, Chimborazo. Online, find articles about Richmond's prisons and the battles fought near the city.

Antietam National Battlefield
Sharpsburg, Maryland
nps.gov/anti/index.htm

At the park and on its website, find information about September 17, 1862, the bloodiest day in American history, when 23,000 soldiers were wounded, killed, or listed as missing in just twelve hours. Take the virtual tour of the battlefield. Watch a video of artillery firing, and learn why so many men were killed by these weapons. View thirty photographs taken by Alexander Gardner right after the battle. Read about people involved in the battle, including Clara Barton and Generals Robert E. Lee and George McClellan.

National Civil War Museum
Harrisburg, PA 17103
nationalcivilwarmuseum.org

Exhibits, photographs, videos, dioramas, and artifacts tell the story of the American Civil War.

ONLINE RESOURCES

American Battlefield Trust
Civil War Trust Digital Collection
battlefields.org/learn

Watch videos and read articles about various Civil War topics, including battles, amputations, casualties, biographies, and the role of women.

National Library of Medicine
"Binding Wounds, Pushing Boundaries: African Americans in Civil War Medicine."
nlm.nih.gov/exhibition/bindingwounds/index.html

Explore an online exhibit about African American men and women who worked as surgeons, nurses, and hospital workers during the Civil War. Site includes primary source materials, lesson plans, and photographs.

National Museum of Health and Medicine on Flickr
"Images related to the Civil War in the National Museum of Health and Medicine."
flickr.com/photos/medicalmuseum/albums/72157614294677868

Check out more than 300 medical photographs of wounded Civil War soldiers, surgical instruments, and hospitals.

PBS

The Civil War

PBS.org/kenburns/civil-war

Discover more about the Civil War in the PBS documentary film originally broadcast in 1990. The series website includes videos, photographs, biographies of key figures, classroom activities, and links to more resources.

Mercy Street

PBS.org/mercy-street

Watch the PBS drama about a Union hospital in Alexandria, Virginia. The program accurately shows the many aspects of Civil War medical care. The website contains additional information in blog posts, short videos, and educator materials. Read more about surgery, disease, nursing, and hospitals.

Smithsonian Institution

Civil War 360.

smithsonianchannel.com/shows/civil-war-360/1003283

Watch short videos about the Civil War, featuring untold tales and items preserved at the Smithsonian Institution. Three examples:

smithsonianchannel.com/videos/the-gruesome-reality-of-civil-war-medicine/22937

See surgeon instruments used in amputations and the prostheses and crutches provided to amputees.

smithsonianchannel.com/videos/the-secret-lives-of-some-civil-war-soldiers/30035

Learn about drummer boys and women posing as male soldiers.

smithsonianchannel.com/videos/how-black-union-soldiers-went-from-slavery-to-forever-free/23094

Find out about African Americans who became Union soldiers.

A wounded Union soldier in a Zouave uniform receives care near the end of the war.

AUTHOR'S NOTE

Blood and Germs is the first book in my Medical Fiasco trilogy. At the start of this project, I was stunned by the Civil War casualty statistics. Yet beyond those shocking numbers, I discovered hard-earned medical successes and advances that saved lives—then and now.

Men signed up to fight for many reasons. Belief in ending slavery and maintaining the Union. Belief in continuing slavery and maintaining states' rights. A sense of patriotic duty. Community pressure. Dreams of glory. The need for a paying job. On both sides, there were men who didn't want to fight, but who were drafted and forced into battle. These personal motivations made no difference to the bullets and microbes.

My research was sometimes challenging. Official records from the Civil War contain errors, not surprising given the confusion of battle. There are inaccuracies in military reports, mistakes in dates, misidentification of individuals, lapses of memory. False information had often been perpetuated for years. Tracking down facts required extensive detective work. I have done my best to get them right.

To determine what Civil War surgeons knew about the human body and disease, I reviewed the medical books and manuals they used. Names of diseases and their diagnoses are occasionally different from those used today, and I referred to the work of medical historians and experts to clarify these discrepancies.

Most of the personal stories highlighted in *Blood and Germs* come from *The Medical and Surgical History of the War of the Rebellion* published by the U.S. Army medical office several years after the war. It documents about 6 million cases of illness and a quarter million wounds. Details about thousands of individual cases, based on surgeon reports, are also included.

I found additional medical accounts in the work of Reed Brockway Bontecou (1824–1907), surgeon-in-charge at Harewood Hospital in Washington. In 1865, to document his surgeries for the Army Medical Museum, Bontecou took photographs of his patients, some of which appear in this book. He intended the images and accompanying case histories to teach surgeons more about gunshot wounds. After the war, patients applying for a federal pension used Bontecou's photographs to prove the extent of their war wounds.

The other patient cases in *Blood and Germs* come from a collection of photographs taken at the Army Medical Museum in the 1860s and 1870s to illustrate surgical procedures. These images are now part of the Otis Historical Archives of the National Museum of Health and Medicine.

I read hundreds of surgeon reports from these three sources, searching for examples of diseases and wounds that would best illustrate Civil War medicine to young readers. Although I tried to balance northern and southern patients, most of the surviving medical records describe Union soldiers.

I included the patient photographs to help readers view each man as an individual, not a statistic. Whenever possible, I searched for background information about them. How old were they? (Many soldiers were teens, no older than a high school senior.) Where were they from? Did they have families? Did they survive the war? If so, what happened to them later in life?

To unearth these personal histories, I started with the surgeon notes. From there, I checked military records in the Civil War Soldiers and Sailors System organized by the National Park Service. I collected additional information on regimental histories from Frederick H. Dyer's *A Compendium of the War of the Rebellion*. To find more background on individuals before and after the war, I used U.S. census and military pension records. For some of the men, I located details about their families and deaths at FindaGrave.com. In a few cases, I was able to use the patient's memoirs.

The story of Civil War medicine also involves the women and men who put themselves in harm's way to care for those who fought the battles— doctors, nurses, camp and hospital workers, and volunteers. To learn about these noncombatants, I read first-person accounts, diaries, memoirs, and speeches. A separate bibliography of personal accounts appears at the end of the book for interested readers. (See page 167). All direct quotes come from these primary sources, as well as from military correspondence, surgeon reports, and journalists. (See Source Notes on page 156.)

In order to put the medical material in context, I studied books and journal articles by Civil War historians. The experts, staff, publications, and exhibits at the National Museum of Civil War Medicine, in Frederick, Maryland, were key resources.

The Civil War was an important turning point in America's history. Its significant impact on medicine in the United States continues today. Through the experiences of those who suffered and those who cared for them, we can still gain insight into disease, surgery, patient care—and war.

— GJ

In May 1864, Union soldiers at a Virginia farm prepare to bury the man on the stretcher, who was killed during a nearby battle,

ACKNOWLEDGMENTS

As I investigated the medical story of the Civil War, the outstanding resources of the National Museum of Civil War Medicine in Frederick, Maryland, were indispensable. My appreciation goes to the staff for providing extensive information and answering my questions. Director of Research Terry Reimer was particularly helpful.

In collecting images and additional material, I was fortunate to have the assistance of the following people who generously provided their expertise: Angelica Blackwell, Exchange Hotel Civil War Museum, Gordonsville, Virginia; Eric Blevins, North Carolina Museum of History; Graham Dozier, Virginia Museum of History and Culture; Annakathryn Welch, Archives of Michigan, Michigan History Center; and the staff of Kroch Library, Division of Rare and Manuscript Collections, Cornell University.

Much hard work and care are involved in producing a book and getting it into the hands of readers. For their supportive and skillful efforts as I progressed from an initial proposal to the finished manuscript to this published book, I thank the Calkins Creek team and my extraordinary editor, Carolyn P. Yoder.

— *GJ*

A medical team cares for the wounded at a field dressing station, summer 1862.

SOURCE NOTES

*Websites active at time of publication

The source of each quotation in this book is found below. The citation indicates the first words of the quotation and its document source. The sources are listed either in the general bibliography, the personal accounts bibliography, or below.

The following abbreviations are used:

MSH — *Medical and Surgical History of the War of the Rebellion (1861–1865)*

OR — *The War of the Rebellion: A Compilation of the Official Records of the Union and Confederate Armies.*

CHAPTER ONE
"A DAY OF WAR AND BLOODSHED" (PAGE 11)

"A Day of War . . .": Apperson, diary entry, July 21, 1861, p. 114.

"There is many . . .": Sherman, speech August 11, 1880, quoted in "Columbus Mileposts, August 11, 1880: Even if 'war is hell,' Sherman didn't say exactly that in his famous speech," by Gerald Tebben, *Columbus* [OH] *Dispatch*, August 11, 2012.

"Defeat to either . . .": G. T. Beauregard, "The First Battle of Bull Run" in *Battles and Leaders*, vol. 1, p. 203.

"Shell after shell . . ." and "ball after ball . . .": Apperson, diary entry, July 21, 1861, p. 115.

"the thunder of artillery . . .": Edmonds, p. 40.

"The sight of . . ." and "was more terrible . . .": Hunter, p. 55.

"I remember with what horror . . ." and "and our men . . .": Barrett, pp. 17–18.

"I witnessed the oft . . .": Apperson, diary entry, July 21, 1861, p. 115.

"Men tossing their arms . . .": Edmonds, p. 43.

"The men were lying . . .": Frank H. Hamilton, "The Battle of Bull Run: One Day's Experience on the Battle-Field," *American Medical Times*. August 3, 1861.

"he was dying . . .": same as above.

"The retreat then . . ." and "So utterly . . .": "Monthly Record of Current Events," *Harper's New Monthly Magazine*, September 1861, p. 546.

"cast a gloom . . .": "Dispatch to the Associated Press, Monday, July 22," *New York Times*, July 23, 1861.

"a decisive victory": "The Great Victory," *Richmond Dispatch*, July 22, 1861.

CHAPTER TWO
BILLY YANK AND JOHNNY REB (PAGE 19)

"The spirit of these men . . .": W. S. King, "Report of Medical Director King," MSH, vol. 1, part 1, Appendix, p. 3.

"Thousands of boys . . ." and "felt a sense . . .": Bull, p. 1.

"No one stopped . . .": Hunter, p. 18.

"I could only thank . . .": Edmonds, pp. 20–21.

"the aged . . .": Charles S. Tripler, "Report of Medical Director Tripler," MSH, vol. 1, part 1, Appendix, p. 47.

"We have come to the end . . ." and "except we wait . . .": Mrs. Gibson, quoted by Chesnut, diary entry, June 4, 1862, p. 174.

"All were accepted . . .": Hunter, p. 18.

"by robbing the . . .": Chesnut, diary entry, September 24, 1864, p. 327.

"a perfect nuisance": J. Franklin Dyer, journal entry, June 19, 1864, p. 174.

"Drummer-Boy . . .": "Marriage of the Drummer-Boy of Chickamauga," *New York Times*, May 25, 1875.

CHAPTER THREE
BUGS, PARASITES, AND MICROBES (PAGE 26)

"Where balls have . . .": Chisolm, p. 121.

"Disease is the fell . . . " and "To keep an army . . .": Chisolm, 1864, p. 121.

"proved so fatal in camp . . .": Professor Paul F. Eve, quoted in MSH, vol. 1, part 3, p. 649.

"We are dying faster . . .": letter from T. G. A. to Mary Livermore, January 18, 1862, in Livermore, p. 642.

"crawling made . . .": Hunter, 279.

"these pests . . .": Hunter, 280.

"The other day I could not . . .": letter from Mary Phinney, Baroness von Olnhausen, May 21, 1865, in Munroe, pp. 203–04.

CHAPTER FOUR
THE VIRGINIA QUICKSTEP (PAGE 37)

"We have a great deal . . .": letter from Lee to wife, September 1, 1861, in Lee, p. 43.

"Cleanliness of the encampment . . .": Chisolm, p. 123.

"The air is poisoned . . .": Woodward, p. 50.

"nothing was found . . .": report of Assistant Surgeon George McC. Miller, MSH, vol. 1, part 2, p. 136.

"It is almost impossible . . .": J. Franklin Dyer, journal entry, July 7, 1862, p. 29.

"symptoms of scurvy . . .": message from Lee to Hon. James A. Seddon, Confederate Secretary of War, March 27, 1863, OR, series 1, vol. 25, part 2, ch. 37, p. 687.

"Whenever we stop . . .": letter from Spencer Glasgow Welch to wife, August 18, 1862, p. 20.

"The Federal troops . . .": Douglas, 144.

"promptly to the requisitions . . .": message from J. Bankhead Magruder to Headquarters, August 9, 1861, OR, series 1, vol. 4, ch. 8, p. 572.

"If a man wants to know . . .": letter from Wilbur Fisk to the *Green Mountain Freeman*, June 19, 1864, p. 229.

"feeling of depression . . .": MSH, vol. 1, part 3, p. 884.

"The state of the . . .": report of Surgeon Madison Reese, MSH, vol. 1, part 3, p. 885.

"In one pocket . . ." and "How are . . ." and "I administered . . .": William H. Taylor, p. 105.

CHAPTER FIVE
ONIONS FOR YOUR SOLDIER (PAGE 50)

"The object of the . . .": Livermore, p. 129.

"that the tents were so . . .": Frederick Law Olmstead, quoted in Stillé, p. 86.

"Don't send your . . .": quoted in Bollett, p. 359.

"Too much praise . . .": Ellis, p. 301.

"Three times . . ." and "and each time . . ." and "to remain in the ward . . ." and "shocking sights . . .": Livermore, p. 188.

CHAPTER SIX
DOCTORS IN BLUE AND GRAY (PAGE 59)

"I had been on the . . .": McPheeters, diary entry, July 4, 1863, p. 38.

"The surgeons who volunteered . . .": J. Franklin Dyer, journal entry, June 14, 1862, p. 25.

"There is a vast difference . . .": Edmonds, p. 372.

"More of our soldiers . . ." and "than from . . .": quoted in Cunningham, p. 253.

"intemperate use . . .": Lowry, p. 104.

"I never saw . . .": Beers, p. 96.

"It is not patriotism . . .": letter from J. D. Benton to his father, October 4, 1862, in Loperfido, p. 7.

"A surgeon . . ." and "having been . . .": Schurz, vol. 3, ch. 1, p. 40.

CHAPTER SEVEN
THE MURDEROUS MINIÉ (PAGE 69)

"I felt a sharp sting . . .": Bull, p. 57.

"The rebels were . . ." and "we could touch . . ." and "Our men lay . . .": letter from Wilbur Fisk to the *Green Mountain Freeman*, May 9, 1864, p. 221.

"A shell burst . . .": Hunter, p. 291.

"We commenced . . .": Apperson, diary entry, July 21, 1861, p. 115.

"They lay in thousands . . .": letter from Z. H. H. to Mary Livermore, July 21, 1862, in Livermore, pp. 656 and 659.

CHAPTER EIGHT
RESCUING THE WOUNDED (PAGE 78)

"It would seem . . .": Bowditch, p. 13.

"Had the medical officers . . ." and "a most mortifying . . .": Brinton, "Account of the Operations of the Medical Department at the Battle of Belmont, Missouri," MSH, vol. 1, part 1, Appended Documents, p. 19.

"to be active . . .": Letterman, p. 27.

"a corps of honest . . .": Bowditch, p. 9.

"filled every building . . .": Mary Bedinger Mitchell, "A Woman's Recollections of Antietam," in Johnson and Buel, *Battles and Leaders*, vol. 2, p. 691.

"The shell fell . . .": letter from John Shaw Billings, May 2, 1863, quoted in Garrison, pp. 40-41.

"with blood oozing . . .": Bucklin, p. 255.

"The air resounds . . .": Thomas Nast, "A Battle as Seen by the Reserve," *Harper's Weekly*, December 27, 1862, p. 823.

CHAPTER NINE
UNDER THE KNIFE (PAGE 91)

"Every house . . .": letter from Daniel M. Holt to his wife, September 1862, p. 28.

"The stretchers coming in . . ." and "their blood-stained . . .": Schurz, vol. 2, pp. 368–69.

"grating of the . . .": Townsend, p. 109.

"The wounded lay in the yard . . ." and "waiting their turns . . .": Townsend, p. 159.

"For six days . . ." and "the tables . . .": letter from J. Franklin Dyer to his wife, December 18, 1862, p. 53.

"I saw large numbers . . .": letter from Spencer Glasgow Welch to his wife, September 3, 1862, pp. 26–27.

"I am covered with blood . . .": letter from John Shaw Billings to his wife, July 9, 1863, in Garrison, p. 65.

"The surgeon snatched . . .": Schurz, vol. 3, p. 39.

"A stream of blood . . .": Cumming, journal entry, April 24, 1862, p. 19.

"As each amputation . . .": Bull, p. 74.

"One doctor carried . . ." and "He would draw . . ." and "I did not go . . .": Gibson, p. 156.

"Floor of operating . . .": Bontecou, unpaged.

"At the foot . . .": Whitman, December 21, 1862, in *Memoranda*, p. 8.

"a body of men . . ." and "I am convinced . . .": Letterman, March 1, 1863, OR, series 1, vol. 19, ch. 31, p. 113.

"first, as to the life . . .": Deering J. Roberts, M.D. "Field and Temporary Hospitals," in Miller, vol. 7, p. 264.

"All day long . . .": McPheeters, diary entry, May 1, 1864, p. 152.

"I was strong . . .": Clara Barton Papers: Speeches and Writings File, 1849–1947: Speeches and lectures; War lectures, 1860s, Library of Congress.

"angel of the battlefield": Dr. James Dunn, quoted by National Park Service, Antietam National Battlefield Maryland, nps.gov/anti/learn/historyculture/clarabarton.htm.

"The surgeons do . . ." and "but no provision . . .": Clara Barton Papers: Diaries and Journals: 1862, December, Library of Congress.

CHAPTER TEN
PUS AND GANGRENE (PAGE 105)

"During the Civil War . . .": Keen, p. 55.

"excessive heat . . .": MSH, vol. 2, part 3, p. 820.

CHAPTER ELEVEN
HEALING (PAGE 113)

"The vivid recollections . . .": Cumming, p. 7.

"Nothing could have . . ." and "This had been . . .": Bull, p. 25.

"The fetid odor . . ." and "was rendered . . .": Livermore, p. 202.

"I spent my shining . . .": Alcott, p. 32.

"The first thing . . .": Alcott, p. 33.

"sickening, dead odor": Mrs. R. A. Pryor, "The Seven Days' Battle,"
    in Underwood, p. 85.

"a bag half stuffed . . .": Hunter, diary entry, May 28, 1864, p. 561.

"The three days . . .": Hunter, p. 563.

"incomparably the best . . .": same as above.

"She was a stern . . .": Mary Phinney, Baroness Olnhausen, autobiography, quoted
    in Munroe, p. 32.

"Blessings upon the . . .": Hunter, p. 563.

"You miserable . . ." and "What do you mean . . .": Bickerdyke, quoted
    in Livermore, p. 510.

"If it was she . . .": Sherman, quoted in Livermore, p. 511.

"who did not fear . . .": Taylor, p. vi.

"A number of men . . .": Cumming, journal entry, May 8, 1862, p. 24.

CHAPTER TWELVE
AFTER THE GUNS FELL SILENT (PAGE 127)

"We did not do . . .": William H. Taylor, p. 104.

"Millions of flies . . ." and "and crawled . . .": Joseph Jones, OR, series 2,
    vol. 8, p. 604.

"We starved their . . ." and "But who laid . . .": Cumming, p. 7.

"The Federal prisoners . . ." and "but our ports . . ." and "could have fed...":
    Pember, p. 121.

"The war and . . .": letter from James D. Benton to E. R. Derry, June 26, 1885, in
    Loperfido, p. 97.

"I have lost much . . .": quoted in Cunningham, p. 269.

"We are tired of war . . .": Walter Kittridge, "Tenting on the Old Camp Ground," in
    Miller, vol. 9, p. 348. (Listen to a 1910 version of the song at library.ucsb.edu/
    OBJID/Cylinder1966.)

GENERAL BIBLIOGRAPHY

Adams, George. *Doctors in Blue*. New York: Henry Schuman: 1952.

Bell, Andrew McIlwaine. *Mosquito Soldiers: Malaria, Yellow Fever, and the Course of the American Civil War*. Baton Rouge, LA: Louisiana State University Press, 2010.

Bollett, Alfred Jay. *Civil War Medicine: Challenges and Triumphs*. Tucson, AZ: Galen Press, 2002.

Bontecou, Reed B. *Photographs of Gun-Shot Injuries*, Volume 2. Washington, DC: Harewood U.S. Army General Hospital, 1865.

Bowditch, Henry I. *A Brief Plea for an Ambulance System for the Army of the United States as Drawn from the Extra Sufferings of the Late Lieut. Bowditch and a Wounded Comrade*. Boston: Ticknor and Fields, 1863.

Burns, Stanley B. *A Morning's Work: Medical Photographs from the Burns Archive & Collection, 1843–1939*. Santa Fe, NM: Twin Palms Publishers, 1998.

_____. *Shooting Soldiers: Civil War Medical Photography by Reed B. Bontecou, M.D.* New York: Burns Archive Press, 2011.

Chisolm, J. Julian. *A Manual of Military Surgery for the Use of Surgeons in the Confederate States Army*. Third edition. Columbia, SC: Evans and Cogswell, 1864.

"Civil War: Images related to the Civil War in the National Museum of Health and Medicine." *National Museum of Health and Medicine*. Flickr. flickr.com/photos/medicalmuseum/sets/72157614294677868. Accessed April 1, 2019.

"Civil War Soldiers and Sailors System." National Park Service. nps.gov/civilwar/soldiers-and-sailors-database.htm. Accessed April 1, 2019.

Cunningham, H. H. *Doctors in Gray: The Confederate Medical Service*. Baton Rouge, LA: Louisiana State University Press,1960.

Dammann, Gordon, and Alfred Jay Bollet. *Images of Civil War Medicine: A Photographic History*. New York: Demos Medical Publishing, 2008.

Denney, Robert E. *Civil War Medicine: Care & Comfort of the Wounded.*
New York: Sterling Publishing, 1994.

Devine, Shauna. *Learning from the Wounded: The Civil War and the Rise of American Medical Science.* Chapel Hill, NC: University of North Carolina Press, 2014.

Dorwart, Bonnie Brice, M.D. *Death is in the Breeze: Disease during the American Civil War.* Frederick, MD: National Museum of Civil War Medicine, 2009.

Duffy, John. *The Sanitarians: A History of American Public Health.*
Urbana, IL: University of Illinois Press, 1990.

Dyer, Frederick H. *A Compendium of the War of the Rebellion.* 1908.
Reprint, New York: Thomas Yoseloff, 1959.

Faust, Drew Gilpin. *This Republic of Suffering: Death and the American Civil War.* New York: Alfred A. Knopf, 2008.

Fitzharris, Lindsey. *The Butchering Art: Joseph Lister's Quest to Transform the Grisly World of Victorian Medicine.* New York: Scientific American/Farrar, Straus and Giroux, 2017.

Flannery, Michael A. *Civil War Pharmacy, a History*, Second edition. Carbondale, IL: Southern Illinois University Press: 2017.

Furman, Bess. *A Profile of the United States Public Health Service, 1798–1948.*
Washington, DC: U.S. Department of Health, Education and Welfare; National Institutes of Health; and National Library of Medicine, 1973.

Giesberg, Judith. *Army at Home: Women and the Civil War on the Northern Home Front.* Chapel Hill, NC: University of North Carolina Press, 2009.

Gross, S. D. *A Manual of Military Surgery; or, Hints on the Emergencies of Field, Camp and Hospital Practice.* Philadelphia: J. B. Lippincott, 1861.

Hasegawa, Guy R. *Mending Broken Soldiers: The Union and Confederate Programs to Supply Artificial Limbs.* Carbondale, IL: Southern Illinois University Press, 2012.

Humphreys, Margaret. *Intensely Human: The Health of the Black Soldier in the American Civil War.* Baltimore, MD: Johns Hopkins University Press: 2008.

_____. *Marrow of Tragedy: The Health Crisis of the American Civil War.*
Baltimore, MD: Johns Hopkins University Press: 2013.

Johnson, Robert Underwood, and Clarence Clough Buel, eds. *Battles and Leaders of the Civil War.* Volumes 1 and 2. New York: Century Company, 1887.

Joslyn, Mauriel Phillips. *Immortal Captives: The Story of 600 Confederate Officers and the United States Prisoner of War Policy*. Shippensburg, PA: White Mane Publishing, 1996.

Joslyn, Mauriel Phillips, ed. *Confederate Women*. Gretna, LA: Pelican Publishing, 2004.

Lowry, Thomas P. *Utterly Worthless: One Thousand Delinquent Union Officers Unworthy of a Court-Martial*. Charleston, SC: Thomas P. Lowry, 2010.

McGaugh, Scott. *Surgeon in Blue: Jonathan Letterman, the Civil War Doctor Who Pioneered Battlefield Care*. New York: Arcade Publishing, 2013.

McPherson, James M. *The Illustrated Battle Cry of Freedom, The Civil War Era*. New York: Oxford University Press, 2003.

Medical and Surgical History of the War of the Rebellion (1861–65). Washington, DC: Government Printing Office, 1870–1888.

Miller, Brian Craig. *Empty Sleeves: Amputation in the Civil War South*. Athens, GA: University of Georgia Press, 2015.

Miller, Francis Trevelyan, ed. *The Photographic History of the Civil War in Ten Volumes*. New York: Review of Review, 1911.

National Museum of Civil War Medicine. 48 E. Patrick Street, Frederick, MD.

Otis, George A. *Photographs of Surgical Cases and Specimens*, Volumes 1–6. Washington, DC: Surgeon General's Office, 1865–1871.

_____. *A Report of Surgical Cases Treated in the Army of the United States from 1865 to 1871*. Washington, DC: Government Printing Office, 1871.

_____. *Reports on the Extent and Nature of the Materials Available for the Preparation of a Medical and Surgical History of the Rebellion*. Philadelphia: J. B. Lippincott, 1865.

Pawlak, Kevin R. *Shepherdstown in the Civil War: One Vast Confederate Hospital*. Charleston, SC: History Press, 2015.

Pfanz, Donald C. *War So Terrible: A Popular History of the Battle of Fredericksburg*. Richmond, VA: Page One History Publications, 2003.

Pry House Field Hospital Museum. 18906 Shepherdstown Pike, Keedysville, MD.

Rutkow, Ira M. *Bleeding Blue and Gray*. New York: Random House, 2005.

Schmidt, James M., and Guy R. Hasegawa, eds. *Years of Change and Suffering: Modern Perspectives on Civil War Medicine*. Roseville, MN: Edinborough Press, 2009.

Schroeder-Lein, Glenna R. *The Encyclopedia of Civil War Medicine.* Armonk, NY: M. E. Sharpe: 2008.

Schultz, Jane E. *Women at the Front: Hospital Workers in Civil War America.* Chapel Hill, NC: University of North Carolina Press, 2004.

Shaffer, Donald R. *After the Glory: The Struggles of Black Civil War Veterans.* Lawrence, KS: University Press of Kansas, 2004.

Stillé, Charles J. *History of the United States Sanitary Commission, Being the General Report of Its Work During the War of the Rebellion.* Philadelphia: J. B. Lippincott, 1866.

Thomas, William H. B. *Gordonsville, Virginia: Historic Crossroads Town.* Orange, VA: Green Publishers, 1980.

Toler, Pamela. *Heroines of Mercy Street: The Real Nurses of the Civil War.* New York: Little, Brown, 2016.

Underwood, J. L. *The Women of the Confederacy.* New York: Neale Publishing, 1906.

U.S. War Department. *The War of the Rebellion: A Compilation of the Official Records of the Union and Confederate Armies.* Washington, DC: Government Printing Office, 1880–1901.

Waitt, Robert W. Jr. *Confederate Military Hospitals in Richmond.* Richmond, VA: Richmond Civil War Centennial Committee, 1964.

Wilbur, C. Keith. *Civil War Medicine 1861–1865.* Old Saybrook, CT: Globe Pequot Press, 1998.

Wiley, Bell Irvin. *The Life of Johnny Reb: The Common Soldier of the Confederacy.* Indianapolis, IN: Charter Books, 1962.

Woodward, Joseph Janvier, M.D. *Outlines of the Chief Camp Diseases of the United States Armies.* Originally published 1863. New York: Hafner Publishing, 1964.

ADDITIONAL ARTICLES FROM THESE SOURCES:

American Journal of Public Health

American Medical Times

Ancestry.com

Annals of the American Academy of Political and Social Science

Baylor University Medical Center Proceedings

Civil War Times

Clinical Infectious Diseases

Clinical Microbiology Reviews

Columbus [OH] *Dispatch*

FindaGrave.com

Harper's New Monthly Magazine

Harper's Weekly

Historynet.com/civil-war

Journal of Southern History

New York Times

Richmond [VA] *Dispatch*

Surgeon's Call

Transactions of the American Clinical and Climatological Association

Transactions of the College of Physicians of Philadelphia

Wounded soldiers outside a field hospital in Fredericksburg, Virginia, 1864.

PERSONAL ACCOUNTS BIBLIOGRAPHY

During the years following the Civil War, many personal accounts of the conflict appeared in books. Soldiers, surgeons, nurses, volunteers, and their family members published their memoirs, diaries, and letters. In my research for *Blood and Germs*, I referred to the following narratives. The interested reader can find many of these and more at Internet Archive (archive.org/details/civilwardocuments [search collection for "personal narratives"]).

Alcott, L. M. *Hospital Sketches*. Boston: James Redpath, 1863.

Apperson, John Samuel, *Repairing the "March of Mars": The Civil War Diaries of John Samuel Apperson, Hospital Steward in the Stonewall Brigade, 1861–1865*. Edited by John Herbert Roper. Macon, GA: Mercer University Press, 2001.

Barrett, Edwin S. *What I Saw at Bull Run: An Address*. Boston: Beacon Press, 1886.

Beers, Fannie A. *Memories: A Record of Personal Experience and Adventure during Four Years of War*. Philadelphia: J. B. Lippincott, 1888.

Bucklin, Sophronia E. *In Hospital and Camp: A Woman's Record of Thrilling Incidents among the Wounded in the Late War*. Philadelphia: John E. Potter, 1869.

Bull, Rice C. *Soldiering: The Civil War Diary of Rice C. Bull, 123rd New York Volunteer Infantry*. Edited by K. Jack Bauer. San Rafael, CA: Presidio Press, 1977.

Chesnut, Mary Boykin. *A Diary from Dixie, As Written by Mary Boykin Chesnut, Wife of James Chesnut, Jr., United States Senator from South Carolina, 1859–1861, and afterward an Aide to Jefferson Davis and a Brigadier-General in the Confederate Army*. Edited by Isabella D. Martin and Myrta Lockett Avary. New York: D. Appleton, 1906.

Cumming, Kate. *A Journal of Hospital Life in the Confederate Army of Tennessee from the Battle of Shiloh to the End of the War: With Sketches of Life and Character, and Brief Notices of Current Events during that Period.* Louisville, KY: John P. Morton, 1866.

Douglas, Henry Kyd. *I Rode with Stonewall: Being Chiefly the War Experiences of the Youngest Member of Jackson's Staff from the John Brown Raid to the Hanging of Mrs. Surratt.* St. Simons Island, GA: Mockingbird Books, 1940.

Dyer, J. Franklin. *The Journal of a Civil War Surgeon.* Edited by Michael B. Chesson. Lincoln, NE: University of Nebraska Press, 2003.

Edmonds, S. Emma E. *Nurse and Spy in the Union Army: Comprising the Adventures and Experiences of a Woman in Hospitals, Camps, and Battle-Fields.* Hartford, CT: W. S. Williams, 1865.

Ellis, Thomas T. *Leaves from the Diary of an Army Surgeon; or, Incidents of Field Camp, and Hospital Life.* New York: John Bradburn, 1863.

Fisk, Wilbur. *Hard Marching Every Day: The Civil War Letters of Private Wilbur Fisk, 1861–1865.* Lawrence, KS: University Press of Kansas, 1992.

Garrison, Fielding H. *John Shaw Billings, A Memoir.* New York: G. P. Putnam's Sons, 1915.

Gibson, J. W. (Watt). *Recollections of a Pioneer.* St. Joseph, MO: Nelson-Hanne Printing, 1912.

Holt, Daniel M. *A Surgeon's Civil War: The Letters and Diary of Daniel M. Holt, M.D.* Edited by James M. Greiner, Janet L. Coryell, and James R. Smither. Kent, OH: Kent State University Press, 1994.

Hunter, Alexander. *Johnny Reb and Billy Yank.* New York: Neale Publishing, 1905.

Keen, W. W. *Medical Research and Human Welfare: A Record of Personal Experiences and Observations during a Professional Life of Fifty-Seven Years.* Cambridge, MA: H. O. Houghton, 1917.

Lee, Captain Robert E. *Recollections and Letters of Robert E. Lee.* New York: Doubleday, 1905.

Letterman, Jonathan. *Medical Recollections of the Army of the Potomac.* New York: D. Appleton, 1866.

Livermore, Mary A. *My Story of the War: A Woman's Narrative of Four Years Personal Experience.* Hartford, CT: A. D. Worthington, 1890.

Loperfido, Christopher E. *Death, Disease, and Life at War: The Civil War Letters of Surgeon James D. Benton, 111th and 98th New York Infantry Regiments, 1862–1865.* El Dorado Hills, CA: Savas Beatie, 2018.

McPheeters, William M. *I Acted from Principle: The Civil War Diary of Dr. William M. McPheeters, Confederate Surgeon in the Trans-Mississippi.* Fayetteville, AR: University of Arkansas Press, 2002.

Munroe, James Phinney. *Adventures of an Army Nurse in Two Wars: Edited from the Diary and Correspondence of Mary Phinney, Baroness von Olnhausen.* Boston: Little, Brown, 1903.

Pember, Phoebe Yates. *A Southern Woman's Story.* New York: G. W. Carleton, 1879.

Perry, Martha Derby, Compiler. *Letters from a Surgeon of the Civil War.* Boston: Little, Brown, 1906.

Schurz, Carl. *The Reminiscences of Carl Schurz.* Volumes 2 and 3. New York: McClure, 1907.

Taylor, Susie King. *Reminiscences of My Life in Camp with the 33rd United States Colored Troops Late 1st S.C. Volunteers.* Boston: Published by the Author, 1902.

Taylor, William H. "Some Experiences of a Confederate Assistant Surgeon." *Transactions of the College of Physicians of Philadelphia.* Third series, Volume 28, 1906: 91–121.

Townsend, George Alfred. *Campaigns of a Non-Combatant, and His Romaunt Abroad during the War.* New York: Blelock, 1866.

Welch, Spencer Glasgow. *A Confederate Surgeon's Letters to His Wife.* New York: Neale Publishing, 1911.

Whitman, Walt. *Complete Poetry and Collected Prose.* New York: Library of America, 1982.

_____. *Memoranda During the War.* New York: Oxford University Press, 2004.

Wilder, Burt Green. *Recollections of a Civil War Medical Cadet.* Edited by Richard M. Reid. Kent, OH: Kent State University Press, 2017.

INDEX

Page numbers in **boldface** refer to images and/or captions.

PICTURE CREDITS